THREE D – GRAPHIC SPACES

GERRIT TERSTIEGE EDITOR

THREE D
GRAPHIC
SPACES

WITH CONTRIBUTIONS BY STEVEN HELLER
AND STEFAN SAGMEISTER

BIRKHÄUSER · BASEL · BOSTON · BERLIN

CONTENTS THREE D GRAPHIC SPACES

→ <u>**PREFACE**</u> <u>GERRIT TERSTIEGE</u>

A MAN SITS AT AN OPEN WINDOW IN A NEW YORK HIGH-RISE. HE HOLDS A SIGN BEARING A SINGLE WORD: OVER. IS HE ANNOUNCING THE END OF THE WORLD? OR IS HE ABOUT TO JUMP?
THE MAN IN QUESTION IS THE AUSTRIAN DESIGNER STEFAN SAGMEISTER, LOOKING DOWN INTO THE ABYSS FROM THESE DIZZYING HEIGHTS AND WATCHING WITH GREAT INTEREST AS MORE AND MORE VEHICLES GATHER DOWN BELOW AT THE FOOT OF THE EMPIRE STATE BUILDING. FIRE TRUCKS, AMBULANCE, POLICE, AND THE FBI. AT FIRST, HE HAS NO IDEA THAT ALL THIS ACTIVITY MIGHT BE IN ANY WAY RELATED TO HIM. AFTER ALL, HE IS SIMPLY TAKING ONE OF HIS DIARY EN-TRIES—»OVER TIME I GET USED TO EVERYTHING AND START TAKING IT FOR GRANTED«—AND STAGING IT AS A VISUAL SCENARIO. THE VARIOUS WORDS OF THIS TRUISM ARE EACH ILLUSTRATED THROUGH A DIFFERENT SCENIC ACTION. FOR ONE WORD, HE SWIMS ACROSS THE HUDSON RIVER; FOR ANOTHER HE LIES NAKED FROM THE WAIST UP, COVERED IN BEES: SEDUCED BY HONEY, THEY GATHER IN A CLUSTER AND FORM THE WORD »IT«.
AND THIS, PRECISELY, IS THE THEME OF THIS BOOK: THE TRANS-POSITION OF MESSAGES INTO THREE-DIMENSIONAL STAGED SCENES. THE EXAMPLES COLLECTED IN THIS PUBLICATION OF INTERNATIONAL, PREDOMINANTLY YOUNG, DESIGNERS RANGE FROM SMALL-FORMAT STILL LIFE TO LARGE INSTALLATION;

SOMETIMES THEY LEAVE THE SAFE HAVEN OF THE STUDIO BEHIND AND CONSTRUCT LETTERS, NUMBERS, AND SYMBOLS FROM ANY KIND OF MATERIAL IMAGINABLE, BREATHING LIFE INTO THE WORLD OF OBJECTS—AFTER ALL, THIS IS THE MEANING, PURE AND SIMPLE, OF THE TERM ANIMATION.
THIS BOOK HAS BEEN INSPIRED, AND ITS CONTENT CO-DEVELOPED AND DESIGNED, BY CATRIN ALTENBRANDT AND ADRIAN NIESSLER, PARTNERS IN THE PIXELGARTEN DESIGN STUDIO IN FRANKFURT. HIGHLY ACCLAIMED AND MUCH SOUGHT AFTER, THESE DESIGNERS CREATE SUCH GRAPHIC SPACES THEMSELVES, AND TRANSFORM THEM INTO MAGAZINE TITLES, ILLUSTRATIONS AND POSTERS. IN 2007, THE EDITORS AT THE EUROPEAN DESIGN MAGAZINE »FORM« LAUNCHED A COMPETITION CALLING ON DESIGN STUDENTS IN GERMANY, AUSTRIA AND SWITZERLAND TO CREATE A COVER FOR THEIR 50TH ANNIVERSARY EDITION. THE DUO FROM PIXELGARTEN ENTERED THE WINNING ENTRY IN A FIELD OF MORE THAN THREE HUNDRED SUBMISSIONS AND ALSO DESIGNED A POSTER AND A FIVE-PAGE ILLUSTRATED SERIES FOR THE SAME EDITION (SHOWN ON PAGE 6). EVEN THEN, ALTENBRANDT AND NIESSLER MANIPULATED THE REAL SPACE OF THEIR STUDIO WITH VARIOUS INTERVENTIONS, CAUSING STYLIZED PLANTS TO SPROUT FROM A CONCRETE FLOOR OR PUFFS OF CLOUD TO PASS IN FRONT OF THE WALL IN THEIR WORKSPACE. THEY HAVE CONTRIBUTED GREATLY TO THIS PUBLICATION THANKS TO THEIR NUMEROUS CONTACTS IN THE EUROPEAN AND AMERICAN DESIGN SCENE; THEY HAVE ENRICHED ITS CONTENT AND TRANSFORMED IT INTO AN INSPIRING VISUAL COMPENDIUM. I WOULD LIKE TO EXPRESS MY DEEP GRATITUDE TO THEM.

SOPHIA MUCKLE, A JOURNALIST FROM FREIBURG, GERMANY, HAS PROVIDED KNOWLEDGEABLE AND INFORMATIVE INTRODUCTIONS FOR THE INDIVIDUAL CHAPTERS. IN 2005 MUCKLE, WHO LIKE ALTENBRANDT AND NIESSLER STUDIED AT THE ACADEMY OF ART AND DESIGN OFFENBACH, WAS AWARDED THE »WILHELM BRAUN-FELDWEG PRIZE FOR CRITICAL WRITING IN THE FIELD OF DESIGN« FOR HER PUBLICATION TITLED »SEINS FICTION«. AND, LAST BUT NOT LEAST, I AM ESPECIALLY THRILLED TO HAVE THE PRIVILEGE OF A CONTRIBUTION BY STEVEN HELLER, WHO ILLUMINATES THE HISTORICAL DIMENSION OF THIS TOPIC. AS ART DIRECTOR FOR THE »NEW YORK TIMES BOOK REVIEW« FOR MANY YEARS, STEVEN HELLER HARDLY REQUIRES ANY INTRODUCTION: THE AUTHOR AND EDITOR OF MORE THAN A HUNDRED PUBLICATIONS ON THE HISTORY AND CONTEMPORARY ISSUES OF GRAPHIC DESIGN, HE IS REGARDED AS AN INTERNATIONAL AUTHORITY IN THE FIELD AND IS A FAMILIAR FIGURE TO DESIGNERS ON BOTH SIDES OF THE ATLANTIC THROUGH HIS WORK AT THE NEW YORK SCHOOL OF VISUAL ARTS, AS WELL AS HIS NUMEROUS JOURNAL ARTICLES AND LECTURES.

WELL, STEFAN SAGMEISTER DID NOT JUMP FROM THE WINDOW OF THE EMPIRE STATE BUILDING, NOR WAS HE ARRESTED BY THE FBI. THE DREAMS, THEMES, AND SCHEMES THAT INSPIRED HIM TO TRANSLATE HIS DIARY ENTRIES INTO THREE-DIMENSIONAL SCENARIOS ARE REVEALED IN AN INTERVIEW THAT COMPLETES THIS BOOK, AND I WOULD ALSO LIKE TO EXPRESS MY HEARTFELT THANKS TO HIM.

Gerrit Terstiege (40) is the Editor-in-Chief of »form« and has worked on the last seventy issues of the design magazine, since 1997. Terstiege is also active in teaching. He has lectured at the design universities in Karlsruhe, Zürich, and Basel and has taught as a visiting professor at the University of Applied Sciences in Mainz. www.form.de

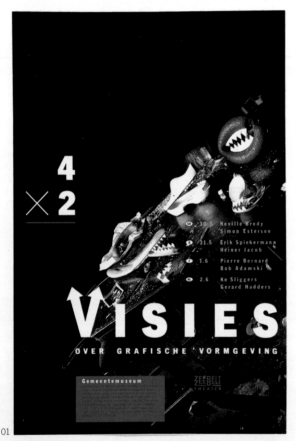

01

02

STEVEN HELLER
ILLUSIONISM MEETS DIMENSIONALISM

Who could possibly be immune to the sensuous wiles of Meret Oppenheim's 1936 »Fur Cup«? Without doubt, it has influenced countless artists and designers who currently create dimensional illusions. It is the gold standard of transforming the real into the surreal—of making something seem entirely plausible when, in fact, it is the complete opposite. The »Fur Cup« is, let's say, the godfather, godmother, and godhead of what I like to call illusionism.

What is illusionism, you ask? In art, it is a kind of visual trickery in which painted forms seem to be real. A lot of early- to mid-twentieth century art was rooted in visual trickery and tomfoolery—take surrealism, expressionism, and dadaism, to name the major ones. But there is another kind of illusionism—let's call it design illusionism—and it has to do with deceiving the savvy among us into perceiving that two dimensions are really three, and not just with painted forms but with all manner of plastic art. In fact, creating the illusion of three dimensions in two-dimensional space has long been one of the graphic designer's foremost—and probably most enjoyable—challenges. In the mid-nineteenth century, when type and typography were first employed as tools to promote industry and business, designers created letterforms and images that were intended to rise beyond their flat surfaces for greater visibility. Types with large, massive, colorful shadows and other faux sculptural elements were commonly used on store signs or display windows to suggest dimensionality and draw the eye to the focal point of attention. On printed advertisements and posters, these stylized typefaces gave the impression of volume, depth, and breadth. By the late nineteenth century, what might be called the »graphic design tromp l'œil«,—dimensional illustrative boarders and frames with architectural flourishes—gave everyday print advertisements a classical aura, illusionism being something of a classical as well as a modern art form.

With the widespread use of photography as a prominent design tool starting in early twentieth century—what the Bauhaus master László Moholy-Nagy called a »mechanical art for a mechanical age«—the once limited and intricate means of creating dimensional illusion multiplied. The combination of photographed objects with typography was called »typofoto« and many progressive early machine-age designers employed this method to achieve a Modern esthetic while evoking a sense of monumentality. The cover for the designer Norman Bel Geddes' »Magic Motorways«, a 1936 tract about the future of transportation systems in the United States, was a prime example. It did not show overt images of cars or highways, as one might expect, but rather presented the title of the book in three-dimensional letters which cast a dramatic back-shadow that clearly spelled out the words. Rather than literally illustrate something specifically future, these dimensional letterforms offered a mysterious futuristic sensation that could not have been achieved using more traditional image-making methods.

> »THERE IS ANOTHER KIND OF ILLUSIONISM—LET'S CALL IT DESIGN ILLUSIONISM.«

01   **STUDIO DUMBAR**
         ZEEBELT THEATER | 4X2 VISIES
Client   Zeebelt Theatre
Design   Studio Dumbar
Photo   Lex van Pieterson
Year   1992

02   **GÜNTHER KIESER**
         JIMI HENDRIX | EXPERIENCE
Source   Jens Nober (Photo) for the
         German Poster Museum, Essen
Year   1969

»WHAT CONTINUES TO HOLD THE MOST WONDER ARE NOT THE VIRTUAL IMAGES, BUT THE HANDMADE ARTIFACTS.«

Where Bel Geddes' book was an exploration of a not-too-distant, pragmatic future, Moholy-Nagy's famous Bauhaus Books experimented with the future of print media. When he conceived his three-dimensional cover for 14 Bauhausbücher, where he composed type on a piece of clear plastic and photographed both the type and its shadow falling on the surface behind it, his goal was to literally add another dimension to how graphic design was employed and perceived. Moholy sought to liberate type and typography, images and imagery, from the strictures of two dimensions, even if in reality the result was still stuck on the two-dimensional printed page. In the same vein, other Modernists, including Ladislav Sutnar, Herbert Bayer, and Piet Zwart, turned to the camera instead of the pen or brush for illusionary purposes—each created designs that seemed to jump off the page.

By the late 1930s, model-making had also become a major element in the designer's toolkit. Building structures—large and small—that were photographed and often collaged or montaged to create new realities was so common that a genre called »three-dimensional illustration« emerged. The camera, of course, liberated designers to freely produce any kind object and marry it to any kind of graphic material. Dimensionality was the next big thing, and just waiting to become an even bigger thing. While dimensional design was commonly practiced from the forties through the sixties (and still is today), every so often there were milestones that changed the standards and altered the rules. Peter Blake's cover for The Beatles' »Sgt. Pepper's Lonely Hearts Club Band« was one such icon. In fact, it was more than just a 3-D illustration, it was a theatrical production of the kind ordinarily seen in stage or film design, but not in graphic design. The »event« required fashioning dozens of life-sized characters out of cardboard as mannequins and placing them in an environment that was photographed. Of course, when it was printed on the 12″ × 12″ LP surface, it lost its real-life monumentality, but it did retain the ambitious graphic quality that, for anyone who saw it for the first time, blew the mind and other senses.

In a much less monumental way, though not less acutely conceptual, Robert Brownjohn's cover for The Rolling Stones' »Let it Bleed« helped to launch the sixties dimensional design trend. After this cover was released, many more so-called rock »concept albums« rolled off the assembly line. Among the most branded were the three-dimensional covers by Nick Fasciano for the rock group Chicago's albums. Each was some tactile object—made from wood, plastic, even chocolate—on which was etched, engraved, burned, or carved the group's swash logo. Dimensionalism (to coin an Illusionism spin-off movement) is in the lifeblood of many designers. The following are exemplars. Many of Gunter Rambow's posters combine real objects, photomontage, and flat typography for dramatic effect and conceptual monumentality (his world globe covered in cowhide forming the continents is a masterpiece of wit and irony). Similarly, Günter Kieser's record covers use surreal

03		**PETER BLAKE**
		THE BEATLES / SGT. PEPPER'S
Client		Parlophone
Design		Peter Blake, Jann Haworth
Photo		Michael Cooper
Year		1967

04		**ROBERT BROWNJOHN**
		LET IT BLEED
Client		ABKCO Music & Records, Inc
Design		Robert Brownjohn
Photo		Don McAllester
Year		1969

03

04

05

06

07

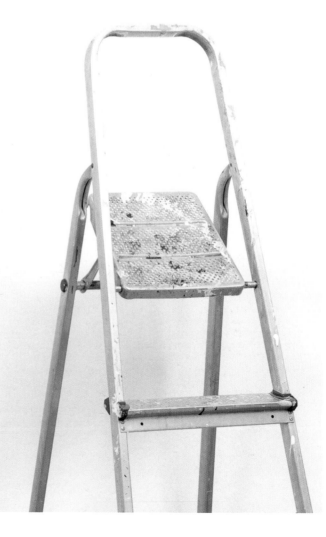

»RATHER THAN LITERALLY ILLUSTRATE SOMETHING SPECIFICALLY FUTURE, THESE DIMENSIONAL LETTERFORMS OFFERED A MYSTERIOUS FUTURISTIC SENSATION.«

transformations of instruments as foils for real content. On an equally surreal note, the design/photo poster collaborations between Nancy Skolos and Tom Wedell set a standard of visual complexity for dimensional art. While these are all elaborate visual concoctions, they don't compare with Gerd Dumbar's elaborations, for which intricate symbolic visual narratives are assembled from various representational and abstract 3-D components and then photographed in a studio, on a table or floor, to create an ambiguous dimensional effect that is at once static and kinetic. The compositions could have been made to look 3-D using flat illustrations, but actually making the 3-D elements was a lot more playful and artful.

Even now, when the computer has made dimensional design, and therefore dimensionalism, so easy, the method still evokes a sense of wonder. But it is not the virtual images, but the handmade artifacts that continue to evoke the most wonder. The handmade method that makes objects seem to have volume, weight, and mass has the power to titillate the eye and mind. The designers who make these illusions are doubtless challenging the perceptions of their audiences, but they are also accomplishing what Meret Opphenheim may have had in mind when she first conceived her iconic »Fur Cup«: she made us look! Illusionism or dimensionalism—whatever it is officially or unofficial called—is the art forcing a second, maybe even a third look—and that's what every designer wants to achieve.

05	**GUNTER RAMBOW**
Client	Schauspiel Frankfurt
Design	Rambow, Lienemeyer, van de Sand
Year	1978

06	**GUNTER RAMBOW**
Client	Egoist magazine
Design	Rambow, Lienemeyer, van de Sand
Year	1967

07	**GUNTER RAMBOW**
Client	Badisches Staatstheater Karlsruhe
Design	Gunter Rambow
Year	2002

Steven Heller (58) is the co-chair (with Lita Talarico) of the MFA Designer as Author program at the School of Visual Arts, New York. He is a columnist for the »New York Times Book Review«, the editor of »AIGA Voice« and the author, co-author or editor of over 120 books on design and popular culture. www.hellerbooks.com

→

STEFAN SAGMEISTER

STEFAN SAGMEISTER
WHY ARIZONA?

IN CONVERSATION WITH GERRIT TERSTIEGE, THE NEW YORK-BASED GRAPHIC DESIGNER STEFAN SAGMEISTER EXPLAINS HOW HE FOUND HIS WAY TO TYPOGRAPHIC INSTALLATIONS, WHAT FASCINATES HIM ABOUT FILMMAKING, AND HOW EVEN ONION RINGS CAN TAKE ON REFERENTIAL MEANING.

GERRIT TERSTIEGE: Stefan, looking at your creative development, one is struck by the fact that you emphasized the spatial, the tangible, in your sketches very early on. Often you move into the third dimension in some way and in doing so lend a certain physicality to a graphic statement, whether with perforations and cutouts, with foldouts, with sliding transparent sleeves, with small chains, or with postcards that can be transformed into sundials when stuck together. What do you find appealing about the object in graphic design?

»I FIND IT APPEALING TO GO TO THE LIMITS OF THE MEDIUM, WHETHER IT'S A BUSINESS CARD OR AN ADVERTISING COLUMN.«

STEFAN SAGMEISTER: Two important points occur to me about that. First, I find it exciting to pull the viewer into the design. Sometimes he or she has to do something with the piece before its significance is revealed. Second, I find it appealing to go to the limits of the medium, whether it's a business card or an advertising column. Limits can certainly be inspiring. Brian Eno wrote somewhere in his diary that the guitar became the most important instrument in the twentieth century precisely because it can do so little. That in turn led guitarists to explore its limits, something that was never done with the synthesizer, because it simply offers too many possibilities. And the same is true of a sheet of paper. It is so simple that it just becomes appealing to push it to its limits.

You were once asked to design business cards that could not cost more than a dollar each to produce, and, in response to this briefing, you folded dollar bills and had the contact information printed on them. But to return to physicality in your designs: one of your most famous posters shows your bare upper body, into which the Swiss graphic artist Martin Woodtli, who was working in your New York studio at the time, had carved with a scalpel the information for an AIGA conference. Nothing was reworked in Photoshop: the blood was real; every letter hurt, especially the list of sponsors on your pelvis, as you wrote in your book Sagmeister Made You Look. Wasn't it difficult to return to your daily work after this radically personal concept? How do you go on after such a work? Was it a turning point?

Not really. I don't recall having thought: »So, what next?« First, because in our studio we aren't concerned about outdoing the last project. I didn't think: »So, that's that. Next time I'll tear my intestines out!« (He laughs.) Second, at the time the AIGA poster was one of several projects we were working on. After it, we just kept going. It wasn't a turning point, no.

Even so, there is a clear turning point in your career that began not long after that now legendary image. I can still recall very clearly that in a circular letter in the 1990s you announced a sabbatical, so that you could get some distance from your daily business and have some time to reflect.

»AT THE BEGINNING OF MY SABBATICAL, I WAS REALLY NOT EVEN SURE WHETHER I WOULD STILL BE A DESIGNER WHEN IT WAS OVER.«

At the beginning of my sabbatical, I was really not even sure whether I would still be a designer when it was over. I simply wanted to leave everything open. Relatively quickly, after about a month, it became clear to me that film would interest me as a medium. Then I drew up a plan of what needed to be done. Since I had already made a music video ...

... in which you put Lou Reed into a chicken suit ...

Right. So I wasn't entirely naive about how film functions as a medium. So I made up a kind of ten-year plan: that was how much time I thought it would take me to make something that I would like myself. And initially I was very enthusiastic about the possibility of working myself into a completely new world, to make films, to spend ten years learning. But then at some point I thought: »What happens if I discover after ten years that I have nothing to say in that medium?«

Not a nice thought!

No, not really. (Laughs.) After all, film is a language, just as graphic design is a language. And I thought: »Perhaps I should use the language I have already mastered and see whether I have something to say with that, rather than throwing away the language I know and learning a new one, when I don't even know whether I have something to say with it.«

ANNI KUAN
HAPPILY INVITES YOU TO PREVIEW THE
FALL AND WINTER 2005 COLLECTION AT
THE FASHION COTERIE FROM SUNDAY,
FEB 27TH TO TUESDAY, MAR 1ST 2005,
PIER 90, BOOTH 622, NEW YORK CITY

The intense reflection on your own work during your sabbatical led to your series »Things I Have Learned in My Life So Far«, which presents graphic design and typography spatially to an extent previously unknown. For me, it makes clear how much you have been occupied with forms of filmic expression, with the esthetic of American cinema. There are stills, short cuts, storyboards, and event trailers for films in which typographic still lives play the lead role. You render individual words or parts of truisms using everyday objects. The crucial thing is that they are not communications or claims from some company, but your own insights and messages. Sentences like »Being not truthful works against me.« Or: »Thinking life will be better in the future is stupid. I have to live now.« How did you develop the content of this series? How did you come up with the particular sentences?

It was just a list I had written down in my diary at the time. Quite snappy. The content remained essentially the same, without any big revision. At first there were twelve sentences, and now they are around twenty.

And in the meanwhile you have staged them all in space?

Yes, exactly.

Some of them were quite elaborate productions. To ask a very pragmatic question: do you finance such works yourself?

No, for each of these sessions there was a specific client. Very soon after my time off ended, an editor from the magazine »Dot.Copy« called and offered me the opportunity to design six double-page spreads however I wished. A carte blanche. »Everything I do always comes back to me«: that was the first sentence I rendered spatially. That was the beginning. I hadn't really expected any feedback on it, but a surprisingly large number of requests came from people who wanted the sentence as a poster. Right after that we received an offer to continue the series in Paris, this time as poster walls—and once again we had a carte blanche. So we did the next sentence in the diary list: »Trying to look good limits my life.« So we flew to Arizona, and every day we formed one part of the sentence from material that was lying around there and photographed it.

But why in Arizona? Why cactus branches? Or, to put it another way: how do form and content relate here?

From the beginning, for me the series was not about a direct connection of form and content. I wanted to leave the connections more open, precisely because the

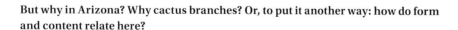

statements are so clear and direct, and, by the way, they are not intended cynically or ironically. Setting the sentence »Everything I do always comes back to me« as a circle or as some kind of Möbius strip would be very »graphic designy« and very shallow. I was never a big fan of ambiguity in design. There are specific references here and there, but they are so personal that probably no one can decipher them. For example, I set the words »I do« with onion rings because Tibor Kalman had an onion ring collection.

In his refrigerator?

No, he dried them and placed them on his bookshelf. So I certainly didn't want to make overly direct translations or correspondences of form and content.

That sort of thing was very popular in the graphic art of the 1970s: the Concrete Poetry of the 1950s brought to the level of design. Just visual puns.

Yes, exactly. Setting the word »rise« with letters that rise from the baseline. You can't do that sort of thing anymore. In principle, every single sentence in this series has a system and rules and a strategy. But the formal strategy changes from sentence to sentence.

And so why Arizona?

There were purely pragmatic reasons. I knew I wanted to be outdoors, in nature. And because it was February, it had to be someplace warm. I certainly didn't want to spend the entire day outside in Alaska. And because there wasn't a big budget, it had to be a place where we knew people we could stay with. And of course I knew from other trips that the landscape there is pretty nice.

What distinguishes the series from art?

For me, it's clearly not high art, but rather graphic design, precisely because every work was developed for a specific client, whether it was a magazine, a university, or the City of Paris.

In addition to the »Things I Have Learned« series, in recent years you have conceived a number of large-format, mobile objects intended to shake up the American public with clear political statements. I am thinking, for example, of the car in the shape of a giant pig, pulling a variety of smaller pigs behind it, whose proportions reflect the ratio of the American military budget to spending on education and health in the United States. Or two school buses, one welded on the roof of the other to form a curious double-decker bus, in order to call for doubling the budget for education in the United States. The idea is very clear

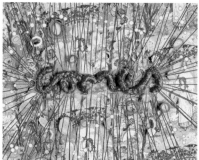

»I WAS NEVER A BIG FAN OF AMBIGUITY IN DESIGN.«

graphically and eye-catching, and it could function as a sticker or poster, but it probably develops the greatest effectiveness and symbolic power in its real, three-dimensional realization as a motorized, bright yellow emblem.

You are referring to our works for True Majority. As a client, True Majority is open to trying out different things. We have done quite a lot for them in the last seven years that didn't work! With such actions, there are always clearly verifiable objectives that are either achieved or not: either a certain number of new members, reports in the media, a given number of signatures, and so on. Often we didn't achieve these goals because the costs of an action were too high for what was ultimately achieved. Frequently, too, though, we far exceeded our targets. The mobiles you mentioned —the pigs and the buses—functioned extremely well. And they still do!

How do you explain their success?

They function so well because they are interesting enough as visual symbols that the American media will report on them. They have been shown on hundreds of TV shows thus far, especially on the local cable news of the cities they happened to be passing through. Because of their curious form, newscasters were inspired to explain what they were about, what they represent. And that always represented publicity for our cause. For a time True Majority was also placing full-page ads in the »New York Times«, but naturally they are only effective for a day. And one of these vehicles costs about as much to realize as a full-page ad in the »New York Times«. And the pigs have been driving around for five years now, and the school bus for a year. This year, when a new American president will be elected, the chances are quite good that the military budget will indeed be reduced.

Which could make the communicative power of the three-dimensional in graphic design wonderfully evident! Many thanks for the conversation, Stefan.

→

STILL LIFES COME ALIVE

Letters dangle loosely from a megaphone with a knitted cover, suspended casually between hazelnut branches: although German designer Juliette Tinnus [→ p. 68] may cause some confusion with the combination of objects as a pictorial arrangement, the scene has considerable charm. Pierre Vanni's [→ p. 57] folded objects, conversely, reprise familiar motifs from painting. Although the three-dimensional objects are constructed from paper, the faceted skull—a garish yellow—and the overthrown goblet, as well as the apple and pear, can all be allocated to the classic repertoire of the still life. But what do the small cardboard machines, which appear like miniature factories in full swing, and the megaphone have in common? Without question: we are faced with an abundance of themes, materials, and art-history references. After all, a still life is

more than the mere arrangement of objects; it is also a form of narrative with objects. The composition of objects into images and contents provides a thread that runs through a wide variety of pictorial representations, degrees of abstraction, and styles of working.

The representation of object arrangements is a universal element in the artistic canons of all cultures. Even antique murals and mosaics depict still lifes of grouped eating utensils and everyday objects. In Europe, the artistic representation of still lifes gained in importance in the Middle Ages and the early modern era. The German and English terms are derived from the Dutch »stilleven«, life without movement or animation. In the Netherlands, where sea trade gave rise to an affluent bourgeoisie early on, the still life became a genre in its own right with a highly developed representative meaning in the seventeenth century. Characteristics include a realistic style of painting and the harmonious, yet seemingly random, composition of still or inanimate objects. The objects are taken from nature or from the world of everyday life. In addition to the decorative value of the image, the key lies in the symbolism, for the depicted objects are like a roadmap to reading the message of the image. If viewers are instantly able to recognize the aforementioned objects in Pierre Vanni's [→ p. 57] works as vanitas motifs in painting, the reasons for this recognition lie in the fact that the vocabulary of this pictorial language remains readily accessible.

The pictorial narrative moment is deeply rooted in the tradition of the still life. It seems only logical, therefore, that contemporary design should appropriate this tradition of representing content and meaning. After all, both share the goal of visually communicating abstract ideas.

It is obvious, however, that not all the works documented here are still lifes in the classical sense. At times, abstract symbols must suffice on a narrative plane in these works instead of arrangements of real, symbolic objects. From a distance, at least, many of these works cite motifs to create references to works in the established canon of art history. Thus the works by the Danish designers of Byggstudio [→ p. 36] combine typical motifs such as pearls and gold chains with cables, CDs, and a half-eaten apple into a crossover of baroque opulence and digital devotionals. In another work faces composed of loose

materials are more reminiscent of puzzles than of the reversed images and object portraits of the Mannerist painter Giuseppe Arcimboldo (1526–1593).

Beyond such affinities, the object repertoire of the still life is generously expanded or liberated from limitations. Instead of inanimate nature, the works by Kong [→ p. 28], or +41 //DIY [→ p. 40] arrange a selection of real products and people into living »tableaux vivants« or collages, miniature worlds and landscapes. In all this, the visual recycling process uninhibitedly mixes objects such as pins and rulers with citations from the history of art. The combinations of historic black-and-white images, office tools, and folding maps by Olivier Lebrun [→ p. 66] demonstrate how vividly unusual stories can be narrated with the help of inanimate and plain, everyday objects.

After all, we have just become used to the most elaborate effects and visual manipulations, as designers around the world have settled in behind their monitors. The computer has become established as a universal tool that not only serves as office and communication unit in one piece but also makes it possible to shorten the once elaborate path from sketch to final print. Despite all these freedoms, the variety of computer programs is limited to preprogrammed options. In other words, the field of virtual options limits the design experiments to a delineated terrain.

When we look at Sarah Illenberger's [→ p. 74] hand-knit miniature organs against this background of digitalization, it is immediately obvious that the sensuality and real dimensionality

of these pieces surpasse digital capabilities. Similarly, Kong's [→ p. 28] material landscapes could hardly be achieved by clicking a mouse. Works like these, therefore, allow designers to emerge from behind their computer monitors and desks, sometimes even leaving their offices. The blank screen or white sheet of paper is replaced by a space which, be it empty or occupied, now awaits tangible intervention with new design methods.

But are these methods really new? Isn't the first impression one of a nostalgic return to predigital manual work? Or even a variation on the popular retro approach? One need only compare the seductively glistening assemblage portraits by Elisabeth Moch [→ p. 45] to Byggstudio's [→ p. 37] likeness collages to realize that this is neither a uniform motivation or formal language nor, by any means, a determined opposition to working with digital tools. Instead, one is struck by the impression that the monitor is simply too small for many designers, the computer too limited, and the workstation too lonely to allow these parameters to hamper the designer's personal creativity.

This is not to say, however, that one would allow a radical approach to working without a computer or any other dogmatic ideas to limit the scope of expression. Digital image processing is simply one among many tools employed to measure the scope for action of contemporary graphic design in new ways. Is it still appropriate to speak of graphic design, given the present unruly mix of media, techniques, and materials? Aren't Chrissie Macdonald's [→ p. 58] objects reconstructed in paper more aptly described as sculptures? Or shouldn't the still lifes shown here be classified as staged photography? This quest for a fitting terminology cannot help but call to mind the Berlin artist Thomas Demand. Based on existing photographs in magazines and newspapers, the artist reconstructs real spaces and scenes in paper and cardboard and then presents the images of these as lifesize photographs. Yet Thomas Demand does not view himself either as an installation artist or as a photographer. The difficulty in allocating these works to specific categories may be understood as proof of a new pictorial language, characterized by a freedom that cannot be limited to the vocabulary of any single discipline. Without doubt, the boundaries between other disciplines have long since become blurred as well. After all, architects have been designing furniture for ages, and visual artists have performed as musicians, fashion designers as photographers, and photographers as visual artists. Perhaps fluctuation and exchange within artistic disciplines make room for more innovation than the economic pressures within each professional's own sector would otherwise allow.

Fundamentally, an intelligent approach to designing is evolving into a theme in its own right. It would appear that some of the works featured in this selection also elevate the implementation or realization itself to a theme. Thus the object kaleidoscopes by Körner Union [→ p. 54] at first leave the observer in the dark as to whether the work represents a typical digital image manipulation or elaborately staged realities. The only clues lie in the minimal positional differences among the objects, the wavy background of the image juxtaposed with the razor-sharp outline of the shadows, revealing that the eye—spoiled by air-brush and filters—may be irritated by simple irregularities.

What may be interpreted as playful irony or defiant opposition to a commercial high-gloss esthetic is more likely a fundamental question of attitude for some designers. For it would seem that the design process has almost been forgotten in the shadow of digital perfection. At any rate, unconventional means and obvious traces of execution offer the opportunity to expand the familiar smooth esthetic of digital design. Thus landscapes created with coarsely torn cardboard are confident and casually defiant statements that design cannot be reduced to perfect surfaces. And drips of color on a CD cover prove that the »happy accident« as a design element is as much a part of creativity as the joy of experimentation.

Although the playful appearance of an individual work may disguise the serious nature of these design examples, the knitted cover of the aforementioned megaphone demonstrates that exposing the design process is finally becoming a graphic design technique in its own right.

Text: Sophia Muckle

LOOKBOOK, SEASON COLLECTION »HEART WOOD«

Client: Swatch AG, Biel
Photo: Collaboration of Hansjörg Walter
and Daniel Spehr

A world where fox and ferret toast each other with a glass of red wine surely is a droll parallel universe. The theme-worlds shown here were created for the Swatch Lookbook as a reflection of the various styles represented in a new watch collection. The Lookbook is a reference work, published semiannually. Each edition presents some eighty new watch models for an audience composed primarily of fashion journalists. In deliberate contrast to sober product photography, living miniature land-scapes were staged for this edition. As if these objects had been caught surreptitiously in secret celebrations or acrobatic exercises, the protagonists, engaged in the frantic busi-ness of living, appear as if in a freeze-frame captured in the eye of the camera lens.

01/02 LOOKBOOK,
SEASON COLLECTIONS
FALL / WINTER 2006

Client: Swatch AG, Biel
Photo: Collaboration of Hansjörg Walter
and Daniel Spehr

03 LOOKBOOK,
SEASON COLLECTIONS
SPRING / SUMMER 2007

Client: Swatch AG, Biel
Photo: Collaboration of Hansjörg Walter
and Daniel Spehr

Jetset Girl

01

Power Trail

02

04/05 **LOOKBOOK,
SEASON COLLECTIONS
SPRING / SUMMER 2007**

Client: Swatch AG, Biel
Photo: Collaboration of Hansjörg Walter
and Daniel Spehr

06/07 **LOOKBOOK,
SEASON COLLECTIONS
FALL / WINTER 2007**

Client: Swatch AG, Biel
Photo: Collaboration of Hansjörg Walter
and Daniel Spehr

06

04

05

07

JEAN JULLIEN
↳196→203

MANYSTUFF

Client: Manystuff Magazine #0

»Manystuff« is the magazine by Charlotte Cheetham, creator of the now-famous blog of the same name. For the first issue, various designers were invited to submit contributions on the theme »realism and craft«. Jean Jullien was inspired by this briefing to create a pictorial translation of his working process. Colors, forms, and ideas appear, expand, and develop a colorful life of their own.

Client: Manystuff Magazine #0

SOUNDVENUE II
DESIGNER PORTRAITS

Client: Soundvenue Fashion Issues
Photo: Andreas Larsson
Assistant: Petter Odevall

Can clothes look seductive even without
models? As regards the fashion edition
of the Copenhagen-based music magazine
»Soundvenue«, the answer is yes. Byggstudio combines the works of young Danish
fashion designers into large-format, uni-
quely atmospheric still lifes. However, these
arrangements and the immediacy of their
impact required more processing than the
Danish designers usually employ. In order
to realize the idea of flying clothing items
and accessories, each piece had to be thrown
into the air, captured in a photograph, and
then mounted into a single, combined motif.

BYGGSTUDIO
↳146→201

02

03

01 MY SPACE

Client: Eurowoman
Photo: James Bates

The Danish fashion magazine »Eurowoman«
commissioned an illustration titled »My
Space« for an article on the Internet forum
of the same name. The various streams of
information, entertainment, fashion, and
music that converge on Myspace were represented through materials and accessories. In view of the target audience, objects
were selected that would give the collage
a feminine character.

02/03 SOUNDVENUE I FASHION DJ'S

Client: Soundvenue Fashion Issues
Photo: Andreas Larsson

Although one of the counterfeit images
may resemble British fashion star John
Galliano, the portraits show the Danish DJs
Kjeld Tholdstrup and Jean von Baden, each
associated with a specific music genre and
scene. The idea for the portraits emerged
while the designers arranged objects that
they had collected as research material on
each group in free association.

01

02

03

01/02 **RODEO**

Client: Rodeo Magazine
Photo: Lacey

If the first thing that comes to mind about
rodeo is an image of rugged, dust-covered
men in checkered shirts, the delicacy of
Damien Poulain's paper cubes for »Rodeo
Magazine« will no doubt come as a surprise.

03 **POULAIN DANS LES BOIS**

Client: Étapes magazine

The English meaning of the French name
»Poulain« is foal. When asked to create his
personal vision of the future by the French
graphic design magazine »Étapes«, Damien
Poulain created a miniature fantasy forest.
The only recognizable elements are two
equine figures at the edge of this thicket of
strange shapes cut from wood.

04

04 ILLUSTRATION FOR
UNIQLO PAPER NO. 3

Client: Uniqlo
Photo: Lacey

Be it the distinctive silhouette of a landmark building, a distinctive means of transportation, or a tourist attraction: a few symbols usually suffice to provide a brief visual description of a popular destination. In keeping with this principle, Damien Poulain created visual abbreviations for the metropolitan cities of London, Tokyo, and New York. The images were created as cover illustrations for the Japanese magazine »Uniqlo«.

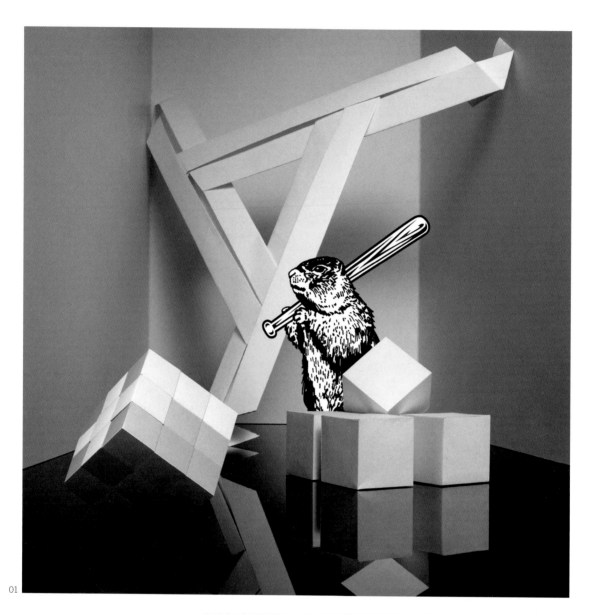

01

01 IMAGE FOR A +41 COLLECTION

Client: +41
Photo: +41

Rather than limiting themselves to specific
fields, the designers of +41 //DIY practice
creative multitasking on many media channels.
Founded in 2001, the design studio //DIY was
expanded in the same year to incorporate
its own fashion and music label, +41. Today,
+41 //DIY create designs for their own label as
well as for prominent clients from the fashion
and music world. The set, reminiscent of a
laboratory and characterized by dimensions
and materials that are difficult to discern, was
created for a photo shoot of the group's own
collection.

02 +41 NIKE ID AIR MAX I

Client: Nike Germany
Photo: +41

Among sneaker freaks, Nike Air Max is an icon.
The first running shoe with an air-cushioned
sole that achieved trademark status, Air Max
has undergone countless transformations and
developments since it was invented. Twenty
years on, +41 //DIY was commissioned by the
manufacturer to stage a visual salute to the
original Air Max.

PARTY NEWS COVER PICTURES

Client: Party News

The design collective +41 //DIY assumed the
tasks of art direction and cover design for
issues 103 to 115 of the hip Swiss magazine
»Party News«. In keeping with their own credo
of never adhering to a specific trend or style,
the visual esthetic for the individual issues
evolved out of the respective themes.

SAROOS

Client: Alien Transistor

Catrin Sonnabend constructed a tranquil land-scape from cardboard remnants, pins, and sil-houettes for a CD cover for the electronic music band Saroos. The band name is taken from a fairy tale about a small people who live isolated in their own world. Imprisoned in the belief that anyone who ventures beyond the bounda-ries of their small sphere must perish, the in-habitants must make do with their cardboard set despite their yearning for the greater world beyond.

01

02

01/02/03 KONFETTI

in collaboration with Mario Lombardo
Client: Spex magazine

Confetti is usually tossed high into the air with
both hands on festive occasions. On the occasion of the 300th anniversary issue of the music magazine »Spex«, confetti was employed in
a completely different manner: tiny pieces
were laboriously cut by hand and arranged by
means of a carefully calibrated and controlled
breathing technique.

04 FRANZISKA

in collaboration with Fellowdesigners, Stockholm
Client: Uppsala Stadsteater

These poster designs in glitter dust were created
for the program of the Swedish city theater in
Uppsala. In her search for inspiration, a creative
spark, and something to lift her spirits, the
designer chanced upon a container of glitter
dust on her birthday.

03

ELISABETH MOCH
↳156→204

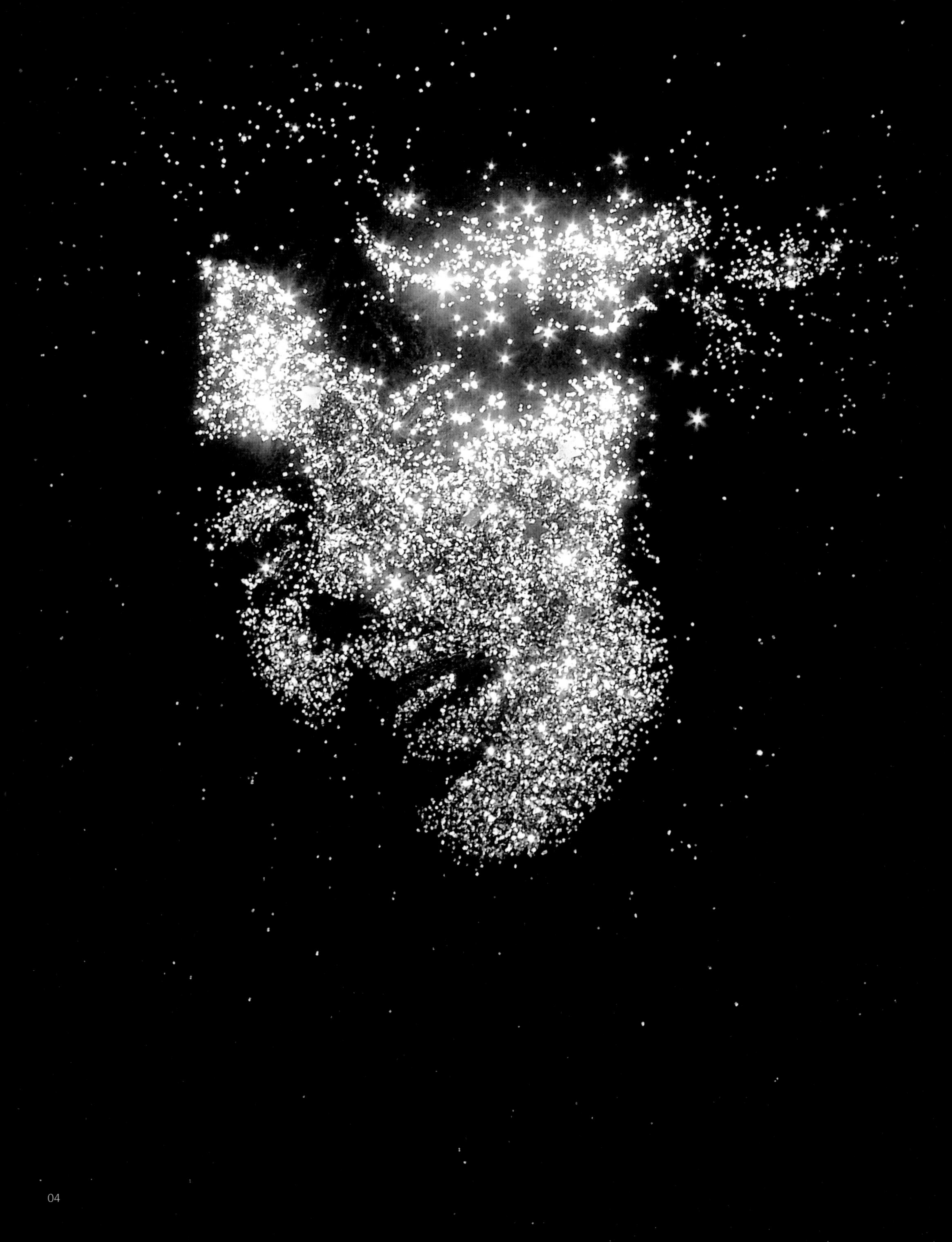

04

NEUSER

Client: Neuser / Universal Music

For the pop/rock band »Neuser«, which was signed under contract to Universal Music before founding their own label »Soundpark«, the Hort designers created a completely autonomous »Neuser world«. Scale and dimension shift within this microcosm. The boxes reflect the music, increasing in size into a full-scale stage set, in front of which the quintet performs their songs. At times, cables morph into a script banner of the band's name. The song titles were added in the form of stickers.

→

»THAT LITTLE HOURGLASS DROVE ME CRAZY«

Interview with Eike König

Eike König (fifth from left); Photo: Rosa Merk

Mr. König, you established your office in Frankfurt about fifteen years ago, originally under the name Eikes Grafischer Hort (Eike's Graphic Refuge). Despite its name change, the »refuge« has remained faithful to its approach, seeing itself as a free space where designers can evolve and develop their ideas. In many works, the playful design process and the fun with the idea are obvious. But if the refuge is like a playground, how do you control the creative process?
The way we work has nothing to do with control. First of all, I have faith in my team. In fact, all I ask is that the works surprise me. Otherwise, what matters to me is that the designers can evolve and develop their ideas here. Naturally that isn't possible with every project. There are large corporate identity projects where there is less room for play, but as long as the project permits it, our work process is quite free.

So do customers go along with that, or what role does briefing play in your approach?
Our customers have gotten used to it, or they come to us precisely because they appreciate our approach, since we try to come up with our own picture apart from the briefing. Since customers often take their lead from other works just to develop rough ideas, it is important for us to get away from these ideas first and discover our own possibilities. Fortunately, our customers are willing to try that.

And how are spatial works created in the refuge? Is a vacuum cleaner incorporated into the design because somebody stumbled over it and then put it back together in a new way?
On principle, we work in teams. Then we talk about ideas until they coalesce into images. And then we start and try things out. Naturally chance can play a role in this phase. But everything is done as a team; there are no set rules.

Do you work with sketches or models?
We work with sketches in our heads, so to speak. Scenarios can usually be described very well in words, after all. The rest is trying things out, and especially with spatial works you have the advantage of being able to design very directly and decide together.

Did you make a conscious decision at the outset to design in space using real materials, and hence not to work with computers?
First of all, we work with computers too, of course. But I studied graphic design at a time when everything was still done by hand. Then the computer came along, and naturally I was excited at first about the possibilities of Photoshop. But in those days the computer took quite a while to perform an operation in Photoshop. When you wanted to move a plane, first you had to think about where you wanted it exactly. Shifting things around took up a lot of time—that little hourglass on the monitor drove me crazy. In the early days, working on computers still had a lot to do with conscious decisions. I miss that today when I am teaching: a certain reflection on your own design work. Today you can sit at the computer, shift things back and forth, until at some point they look »great«. Nobody asks any more why it looks »great« here now, but instead they cheerfully keep shifting things around or go back forty steps by hitting Apple Z.

So designing in real space is a more conscious way of working?
It's about working consciously and a more intense, because more immediate, design. And also about the direct connection to the work—a feeling that nothing can be simulated with a screen in between. It's about formats, colors, setting priorities. The computer per se is a medium with no format. You can zoom in and out, but you only experience the real dimensions when you have an object in your hand. I think that it's still as important as ever to tinker with a work by hand, to try out the dimensions. I even believe that such »real designing« can often be faster than working with a computer. If you work on a computer exclusively, you need to have a precise idea of what is wanted. Otherwise you'll get lost amid all the possibilities.

Interview: Sophia Muckle

WITHOUT TITLE

Self-initiated Work

The experimental arrangement by the Berlin design studio Hort brings to mind the video titled »The Way Things Go«, by the Swiss artistic duo Peter Fischli and David Weiss, who unleashed a chain reaction of everyday things on the occasion of the Documenta 8 in 1987.

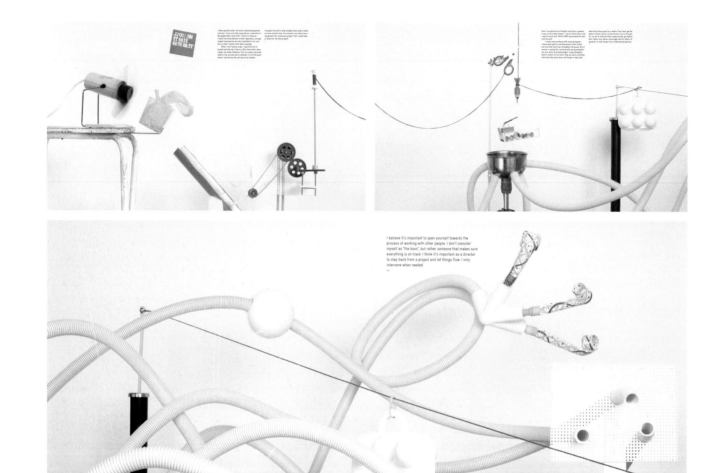

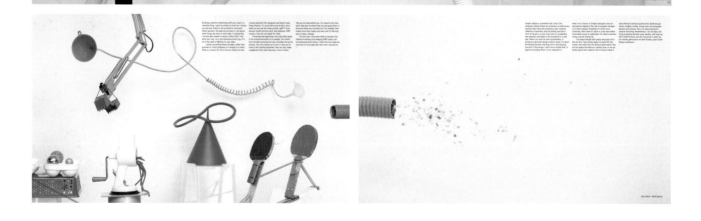

THE HORT INVITES

Client: Academy of Art and Design Offenbach

Seeing the colorful creatures made of play dough assembled for the shoot of a poster motif, one may begin to surmise what the name Hort might signify: namely, a colorful playground for designers, where they can give their ideas free reign. In the context of a foundation professorship at the Academy of Art and Design Offenbach, the poster announced a variety of lectures and workshops.

FACTORY 7850000Z

Client: blond Magazine

The machine park created by Hort in their own studio fulfills two different functions: first, it serves to illustrate questions concerning the future of design. And second, moving boxes are employed in a meaningful, creative manner.

The arrangement of equipment pieces shown here is used to manufacture the colors magenta and Pantone 804, and can be purchased directly through the homepage of the design studio for the preferential price of 162,000.50 Euro.

MAG AWARDS

Client: MagAwards

When black horn-rimmed spectacles are combined with Copic markers and Pantone guides, the designer is engaging in a playful treatment of the clichés of his craft, directed ironically at himself. Taking the typical utensils in each category, Emil Kozak arranges poster motifs for a competition for the best magazines in Denmark.

JULIEN VALLÉE
↳106→186→207

GRAFIKA

Client: grafika magazine

How does one succinctly communicate the creativity thriving in a scene of young designers? Julien Vallée chooses symbolic fireworks made of paper to explode the framework of standard formats for the illustration of the annual issue of »grafika« magazine in Quebec.

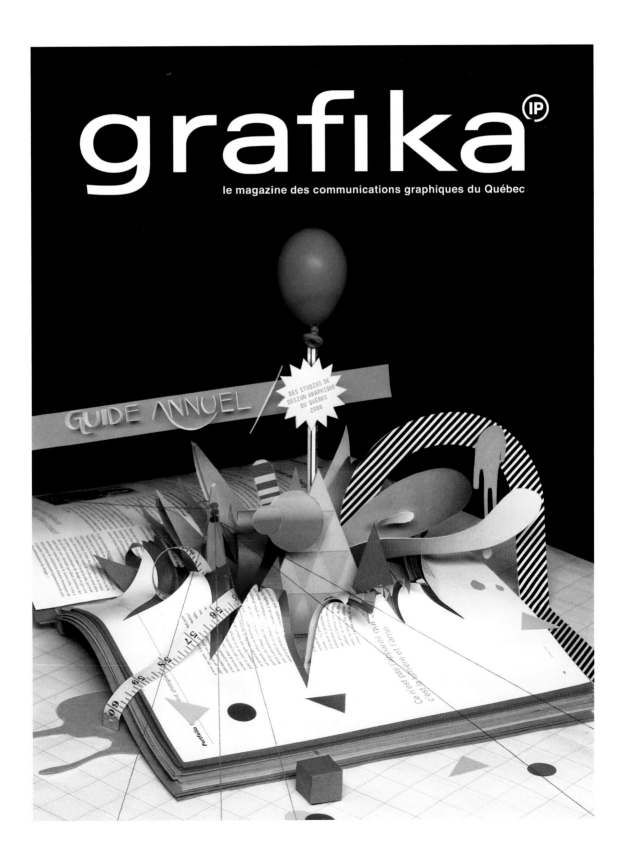

SWISS FEDERAL DESIGN GRANTS

Client: OFC

At first glance, the kaleidoscope images by
Körner Union appear to be an ironic comment
on the esthetics of digital image processing.
For the staging is rendered believable only
through the harsh contrasts, the undulating
background, and the minimal differences in
product arrangement. The images were taken
by way of documentation on the occasion of
the Swiss Federal Design Grant competition.
In order to be able to utilize all the objects for
these large-format photographs, scaffolding
had to be erected in situ at the location where
the jury met for their deliberations.

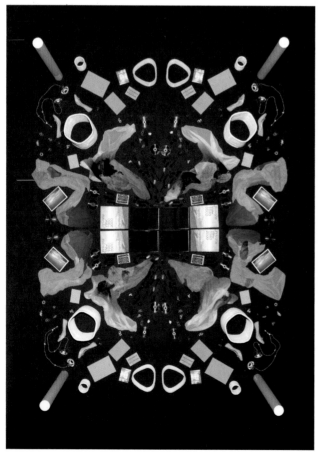

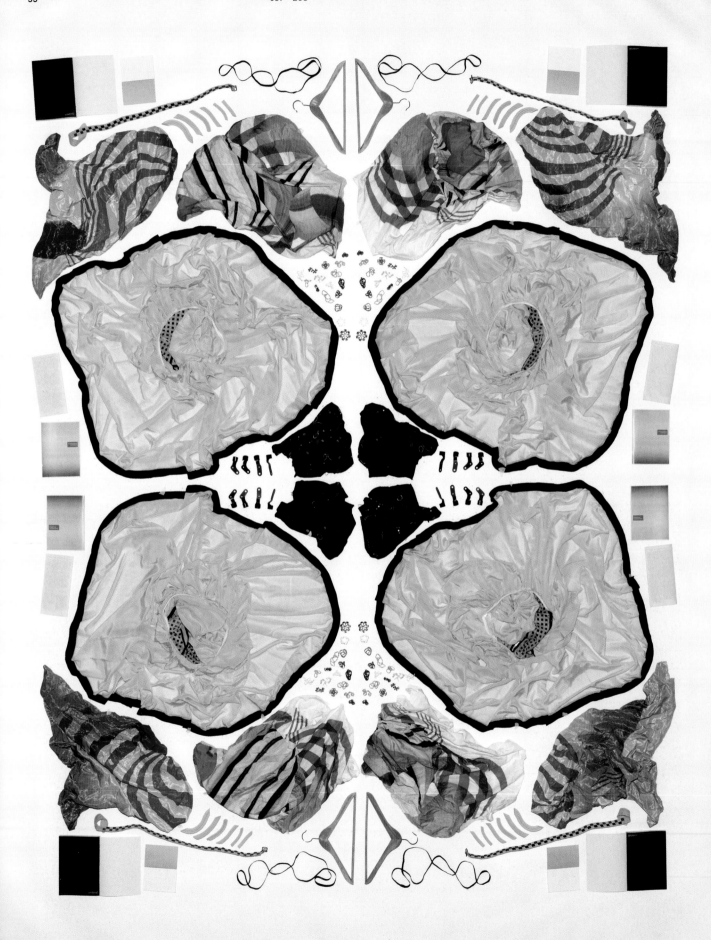

JENNIE HANCOCK
↪142→189→202

MANYHANDS FOR MANYSTUFF

Client: Manystuff Magazine #0
Photo: Jennie Hancock

To render graphic symbols in a spatial manner, Jennie Hancock cut out pictograms
and layered them into a three-dimensional
pyramid for the cover of the first issue
of »Manystuff«, a magazine by Charlotte
Cheetham.

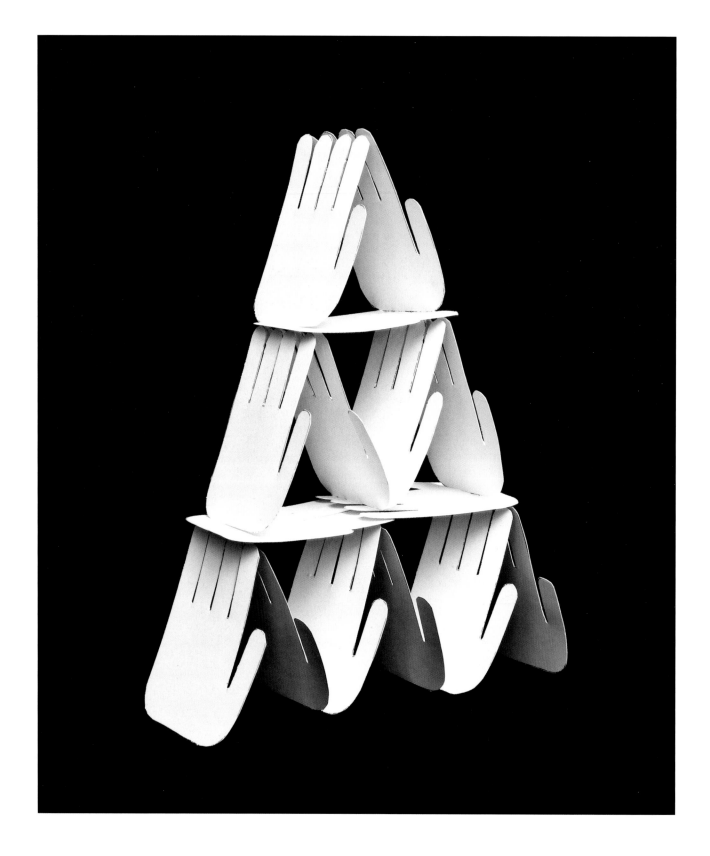

01 LES SIESTES ÉLÉCTRONIQUES
2008 – GRAPHIC RESEARCH

Client: Les siestes éléctroniques
Photo: Pierre Vanni

Since 2001, the music festival »les siestes
éléctroniques« in Toulouse/France has offered
a platform for new electronic music. The free
concerts are held during the day and at night,
in the open air, in museums or in clubs. As
part of the design for the festival, Pierre Vanni
designed a wolf made of folded star maps
to symbolically guard the instruments and
equipment during the nocturnal events.

02/03 VANITIES

Self-initiated Work
Photo: Pierre Vanni

The objects that Pierre Vanni arranges in his
works in the form of paper models, are taken
from the fixed canon of symbols in traditional
still life painting. Despite their abstraction
and coloring, the paper models are also reminiscent of symbolic *vanitas* motifs of death
and transitoriness with Christian overtones. In
his independent artistic work, the designer
explores the transfer of meaning between real
objects and simulation. The title »Vanities«
refers to the art history context.

02

01

03

01 OBJECTS

Self-initiated Work

Chrissie Macdonald's reconstructed paper tools and utensils have the appearance of props from the studio of the artist Thomas Demand. The simulation is only revealed in the apparent sterility of the matte surface and the unusual coloring of the objects.

02 IBM MÖGLICH MAGAZINE

Client: IBM Möglich Magazin/
John Brown Publishing Ltd
Set Designer: Chrissie Macdonald
Art Director: Simon Robinson
Photo: Dominic Lee

Chrissie Macdonald's title illustration for the IBM client magazine »Möglich« (»Possible«) shows a strangely anachronistic monitor. Individual building blocks tumble out of the cover of the empty device; they can—it seems —be rearranged into an analog version of Tetris at the click of a mouse. The allusion to the classic computer game is a reference to the semantics of the game: composing a greater whole from many small individual elements.

01

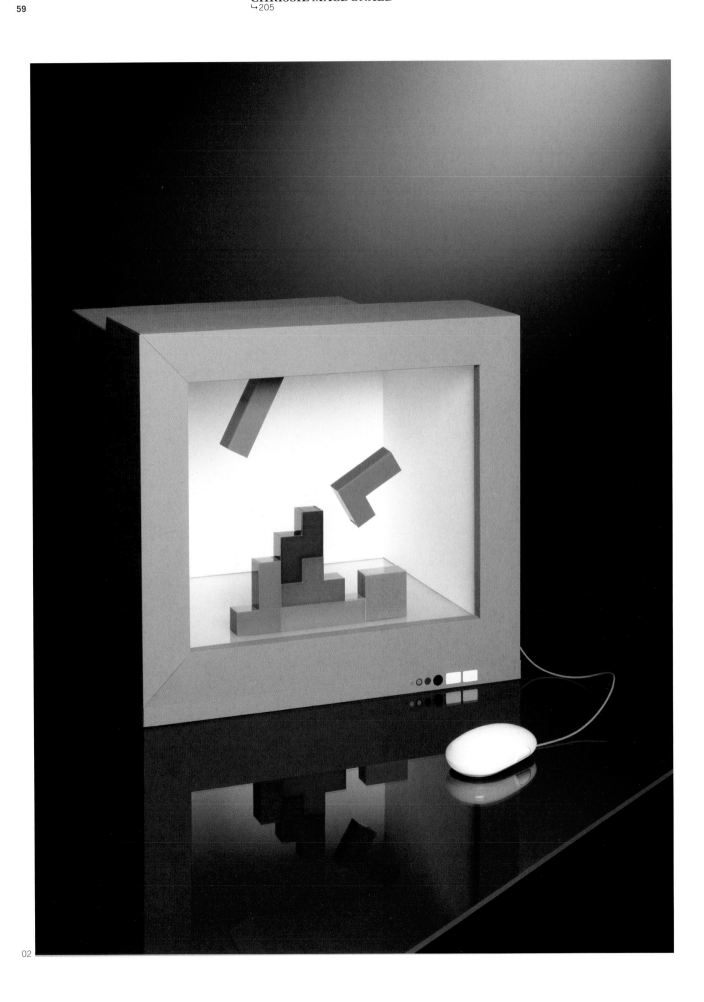

04

03 OVERSIZED EPHEMERA

Set Design & Art Direction: Chrissie Macdonald
Photo: John Short

The tension in the works of British designer
Chrissie Macdonald springs from the depiction
of opposites. Between the polar opposites of
nature and artificiality, proportional scale
and playful enlargement, her arrangements
create spaces where perception is really put
to the test.

04 SMALL PLEASURES

Client: Dazed & Confused
Set Design: Chrissie Macdonald
Photo: Jacob Sutton
Styling: Celestine Cooney

Contrary to the assumption inspired by the
title »Small Pleasures«, the hunt for the coveted
accessories of the fashion industry is portrayed
in the guise of a large adventure playground
for adults. Composed of real accessories and
»fake« athletes, the British designer Chrissie
Macdonald designed a jungle for shopaholics
for the magazine »Dazed & Confused«.

CABANES & CERAMIC BOX

Client: Adrien Rovero

In his still lifes, Philippe Jarrigeon stages a play with scale, space, and reality. Familiar objects enter into unexpected connections, the scale and materiality of which remain uncertain, frequently leaving the observer in a state of puzzlement.

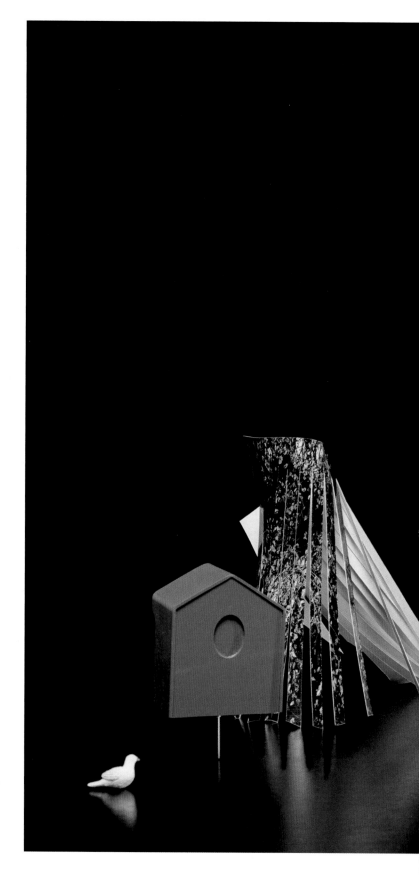

PIEDS DE POULE

Self-initiated Work

Somewhere between surreal glamour and trash: Philippe Jarrigeon's still life with stiletto reads almost like a spoof of Pink Floyd album covers of the 1980s. At any rate, the glass eye framed by artificial lashes belongs to the canon of symbols in an amateurish, puberty-inspired form of neo-surrealism. No doubt about it: it's a statement with a wink.

PANDATONE

Client: Pandatone
Photo: Tobin Yelland
Florist: Saira Hussain

A bouquet and a vase pose for the cover of the Pandatone album »What Has Nature Done for Me Recently«. The design was inspired by florists' calendars from the 1970s. The model quality of the paper flowers functions as a visual emphasis for the subtle irony of the title.

HOMESCAPE 1, 2 & 3

Self-initiated Work

When everyday objects are liberated from the matrix of the familiar box, the most unusual events seem to take place. Olivier Lebrun combines banal objects without symbolic significance into action-packed scenes that appear like film excerpts.

01

01 HERBSÜSS
02 SOUVENIR

Self-initiated Work

The props in the fashion photographs entitled
»Herbsüß« (bitter-sweet) and »Souvenir« are
reminiscent of postcards and calendar spreads
from the late 1950s. The everyday objects and
fashionable accessories by young designers
used in these shots give Juliette Tinnus's still
lifes tremendous charm.

03 SCHLARAFFENLAND
04 HOLLE
05/06 WETTER PHOTOS

Self-initiated Work

The return to handmade methods in a world dominated by technology inspired Juliette Tinnus to create the works »Holle« (derived from »Mother Hulda«) and »Schlaraffenland« (»Land of Cockaigne«). Graphic elements, technical devices, industrial products, and fairy-tale symbols are combined into a strikingly unified pictorial world.

03

04

05

02

03

01 BOILING

Client: Neon magazine
Photo: Ragnar Schmuck

The works in the series »Hochgekocht« were created as illustrations for a food test in »Neon«, an offshoot of »Stern« magazine. Inspired by the portraits created by the Italian painter Giuseppe Arcimboldo (1526–1593), Sarah Illenberger arranged food items into three thematic portraits.

02/03/04 WRITTEN OFF

Client: Neon magazine
Photo: Dirk Eisel

Fantasy cups are created for athletic achievements in disciplines that have hitherto received little attention. The small sculptures fashioned from everyday objects are modeled on typical sports trophies and are slyly appropriate for con men and image-obsessed neurotics.

04

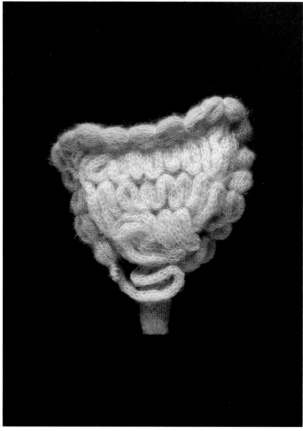

05

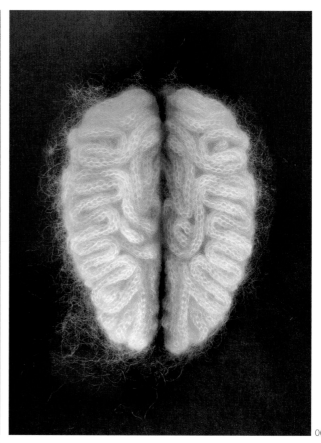

06

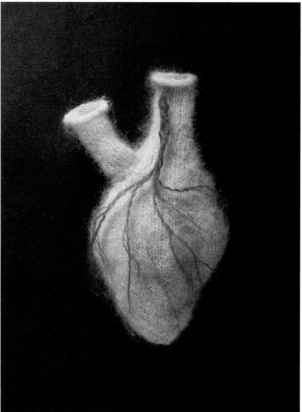

07

05/06/07 TOTALLY SOFT

Client: Sleek magazine
Photo: Andreas Achmann

What might the heartbeat of an angora heart sound like? Sarah Illenberger illustrates the yearning for security in a confusing world with hand-knit human organs.

08/**P76** 09 PEEK-A-BOO

Client: Sleek magazine
Photo: Ragnar Schmuck

Fashion-conscious hamsters and canaries have long dreamed of this: accessories, arranged into an athletic race course. The designer's inspiration for this fashion spread in the magazine »Sleek« came from the artificial landscapes found in zoo enclosures.

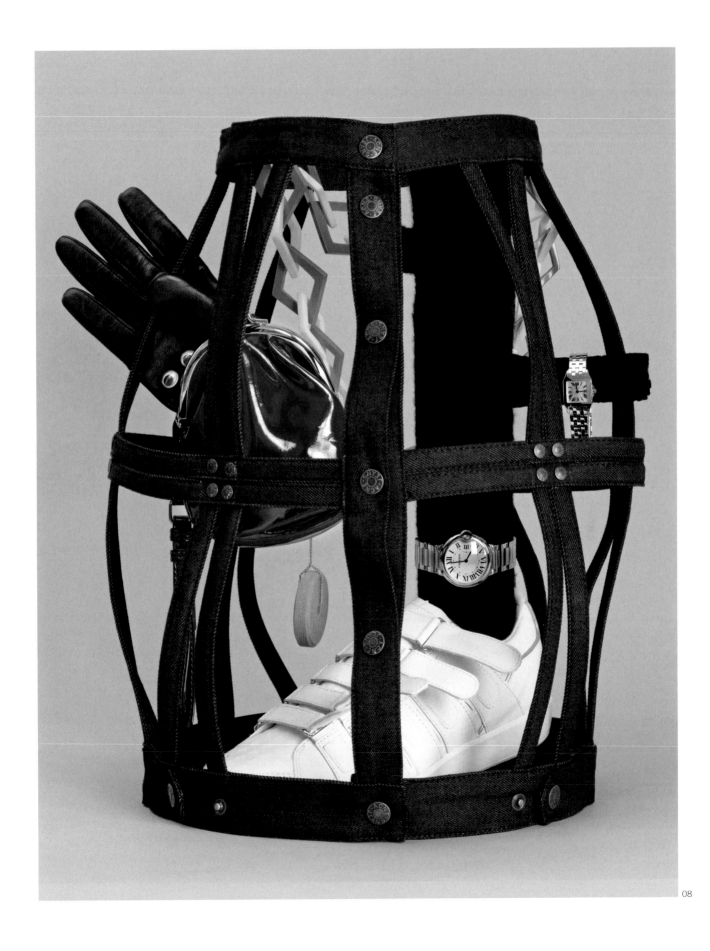

→

INTRICATE INSTALLATIONS

What a white wonderland! A young man in skiing gear looks seemingly into the snow-white landscape downhill. Behind him, the mountain peaks stand out in gleaming white against a dark night sky. One last time, he turns towards the camera before launching on his descent into the valley far away from any groomed slope. The image, which Grégoire Alexandre [→p.90] uses to stage the scene for this outdoor fantasy, plays with established clichés. But just what is it that makes this scenario so different, so appealing? Perhaps we are drawn to it because the mountain peaks in the background are made from paper? Or could it be because the slope terminates in the floor covering of a photo studio in the foreground? The room corner, visible in another frame to the side of the mountain chain, undoubtedly reveals that this is a casual play with illusion and reality.

The question is, what are we dealing with here: art that takes aim at the perfection of commercial images, or advertising that is designed to look like art? A glance through the following pages will reveal that it is difficult to find unequivocal answers to these questions.

Let's take a closer look at some visual examples. To illustrate the topic of freelance work, KatrinSchacke [→p.94] employs her arrangements of office utensils. Each of the puzzling constructs represents an obstacle and a complex of themes, which must be overcome on the road to independent freelance work. This obstacle course could just as easily be presented as an artistic installation or a sculpture in a gallery instead of an illustration in a book. Yet 3-D design is increasingly opening doors onto fields that have been given little attention up to now. Thus the French designers

Antoine et Manuel created 3-D scenes reminiscent of stage sets for the Galeries Lafayettes department store in Paris. At times the store windows are filled with abstract shapes like futuristic transmitter masts; at other times they are decorated with a composition of printed surfaces or with graphically inspired furniture. Eike König's Hort also utilizes the dimensionality of differing spatial planes for his transposition of graphic design in Nike stores. The individual elements of the campaign images are separated out and arranged within the space. The results are changing perspectives with a dynamic impact on passers-by. Considering how drab the usual store window displays can be, the expressive power of such examples comes as a surprise. Although it is worth noting that there have been other striking window displays; in 2006, the Éspace Louis Vuitton on the Champs Elysées demonstrated the happy union of art and commerce in today's marketplace: for the opening, the artist Vanessa Beecroft employed live nude models placed on shelves next to accessories from the fashion label. Quite different is Valerie Sietzy's [→ p. 112] transformation of a highway bridge into a nocturnal stage with the help of bicycle reflectors, which has the feel of a playful intervention in the public space. There's no doubt: between the poles of advertising and poetic street art one can discover unconventional works such as the »octopus of clothes« by +41 //DIY [→ p. 97] or the wooden boxes decorated with prints of historic furnishings by Rita [→ p. 116].

The purposes and applications of 3-D design cover a broad range from illustration to interior design. At times, it seems as if playful experimentation is the most important element.

For instance, in one project by Playarea [→ p. 114], when faced with small robots and the colorful coral mountains, it is easy to forget that the theme focuses on shoes. And the oversized pop-up catalogues by Grégoire Alexandre [→ p. 88] for Christian Lacroix engage viewers in a quest for scale, almost in a classic trompe l'oeil manner, while their attention is all-too-easily diverted from actual content of the image.

When asked about the motivation for or the origin of such works, the answers tend to revolve around the joy found in playful design work within a team. However, the prime attraction to 3-D seems to lie in the immediacy of the material quality and perception. As the British designer Ben Freeman explains, the challenge of direct design is understandable when one considers that we are dealing today with a generation of designers whose idea of design is inextricably linked to working on a computer. When asked what his motivation for 3-D design might be, Freeman remembered his own youthful enthusiasm for books, album covers, and flyers with tactile qualities. On the other hand, he describes how the process of digitalization has increasingly distanced the day-to-day practice of design from such materiality.

Quite possibly, an experimental approach offers the opportunity within the timeframe of one generation to fill the gap between acquired skills and the enthusiasm for real objects. The playful approach that is suggested by the vacuum cleaner performance of Eike König's Hort or the portraits by Eat Sleep Work/Play, therefore masks the entirely serious acquisition of alternative methods of representation and pictorial metaphors.

The designers of the Swiss group +41 //DIY develop a unique pictorial language for each of their projects. This approach, they feel, helps to prevent both formal randomness and, simultaneously, a rigid adherence to certain ways of working and areas or sectors. The name of the group incorporates the collective's own label—+41—which, in addition to independent projects and design work for prominent clients, also produces fashion and CDs.

As sources of inspiration for their work, +41 //DIY cites influences that range from contemporary art to film, literature, and science, thus highlighting a phenomenon that is evident in the most varied spheres of design: namely, the reciprocal influence among disciplines. Take, for example, the dreamlike scenery fashioned from cardboard in »The Science of Sleep«, a feature film by Michel Gondry, the paper stage sets by Berlin artist Thomas Demand, or the homemade paper dresses of the experimental German trio »Chicks on Speed«.

The blurred boundaries between the various creative disciplines provide a vivid illustration of the close relationship between 3-D design and artistic concepts: to what degree is Dada still influencing Philippe Jarrigeon's [→ p. 105] manipulated portraits and costumed objects? Aren't Valentin Ruhry's [→ p. 117] running shoe sculpture and the decorative trim made up of multiple contact plugs ready-mades?

It is interesting to note that the term »installation« was coined by the artists Bruce Nauman and Dan Flavin in the 1960s because these three-dimensional works defied description with the classic art vocabulary. Rather than describing the materiality of a work or the artistic method, the term installation therefore denotes first and foremost the scenic, spatial qualities of a work, as well as their impact on the observer. Installation work is by definition undefined, that is to say, there is an inextricable link between openness and installation, with the latter describing the relationship between the space, the work itself, and the viewer's perception.

Only a handful of the works featured in this selection truly meet this particular standard of open work definition, for example, the 3-D collage by Hvass&Hannibal [→ p.98], which was created for an exhibition. The phenomenon of applied design and independent projects tapping into and utilizing the same scenic and spatial means suggests yet another new term, which might aptly be called »installative« graphic design. The multiplicity of references and themes demonstrates that the works featured in this chapter have begun to translate an expanded definition of their practice into action. While the blurring of disciplines makes classification difficult, the list of references and coordinates in the cultural fabric keeps growing.

There is no doubt that experimentation serves to further develop design standards, methods, and ways of seeing. It is important to remember, moreover, that the global exchange of ideas and digital networking serve as catalysts for this evolution. Although the computer does not play a superordinate role as a design tool in this evolution, it nevertheless enables young designers to develop a new and different idea of self.

Perhaps the »octopus of clothes« by +41 //DIY [→ p.97] with dresses from their own +41 label, suffices to illustrate this change. Instead of choosing a specific approach or field—or allowing themselves to be defined by others—designers have begun to select their own fields or to create entirely new ones. What is astonishing is the formal expressiveness found throughout both applied work and independent design projects.

Perhaps this suggests that clients, too, are searching for an alternative to established advertising esthetics. Conversely, the crisis in classic advertising may very well offer opportunities for those who represent their own design positions in a time of guerrilla and open-source marketing. In the tug-of-war between esthetic subversion and economic collaboration—traditionally a difficult situation—one might at least hope that attitude and individuality will bring, if not wealth, at least recognition and commissions.

Text: Sophia Muckle

LE JARDIN DES DÉLICES

Client: Sleek magazine
Photo and Set Design: Elene Usdin

In her staged photographs, Elene Usdin sometimes tells entire stories in a single image.
Her »Garden of Lust« combines heaven and
hell, and every paradisiacal and nightmarish
sphere that lies in between. Allegories of love,
lust, and death made material enthrall the
viewer. In the tradition of Hieronymus Bosch's
paintings, the cuddly-eerie textile creatures
bear witness to the desires and mortality of the
human body. They are framed by the passion-
ate words of a couple at the beginning and end
of their relationship—a three-dimensional
psychograph.

ELENE USDIN
↳207

LA BARBE BLEUE

Self-initiated Work

The »Bluebeard« series translates human dramas into material form: wool and fabric. Tears become blue skeins of wool; the blue beard morphs into a rampant wig assimilating everything in its path. Inspired by the gruesome fairy-tale of Bluebeard, the king who keeps his murdered lovers in a forbidden chamber, Elene Usdin celebrates the fragility of the female body in a morbid yet enchanting fashion shoot. Twisted real body parts and detached rag-doll limbs combine to form surreal images.

01

ELENE USDIN
⌐207

04

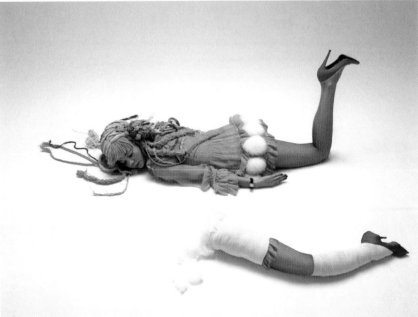

01

01/02 CHRISTIAN LACROIX FOR LA REDOUTE

Client: Christian Lacroix
Photo: Grégoire Alexandre
Set Designer: Alexis Barbera
Model: Lily Cole

The catalogue as pop-up book: In addition to fashion, the Christian Lacroix Collection of 2007 also presents interior design creations. The individual shots were taken in a Parisian photo studio. As if transported into Alice's Wonderland, the model emerges from the pages of an oversized book.

P90 03 ESQUIRE SKI

Client: Esquire Magazine UK
Photo: Grégoire Alexandre
Set Designer: Andy Hillman
Styling: Rhianna Rule

The studio backdrop of the ski jumper for the British magazine »Esquire« clearly demonstrates that paper is a patient medium. The designer's favorite material is piled up into a towering mountain range, the two-dimensionality of which remains recognizable despite the layering. Lined with cartons and other warehouse and packaging materials, which are visible along the margins of the image as if by accident, the model illustrates how the Earth's surface evolved: through folding.

03

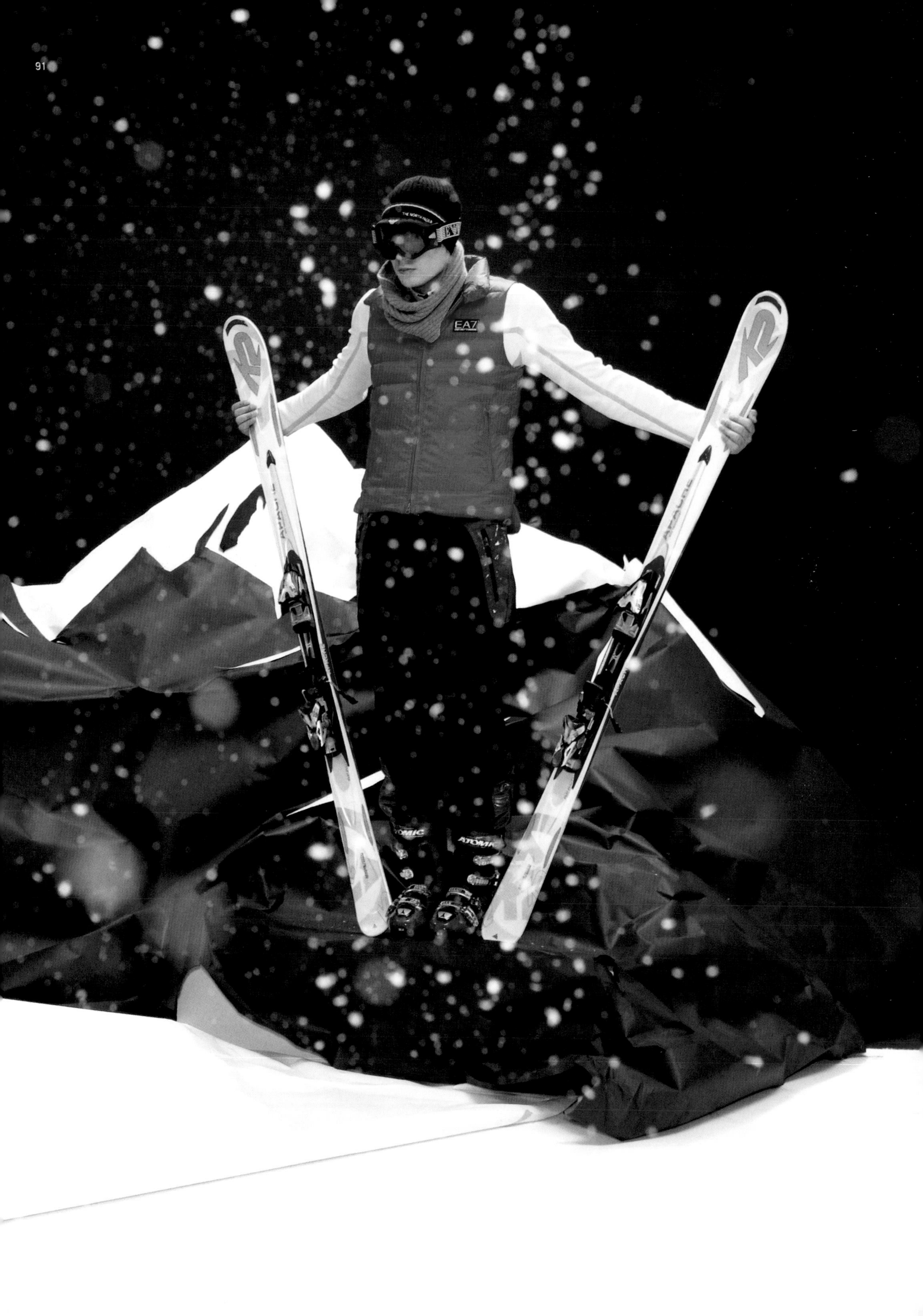
EA7
ATOMIC
ATOMIC

KATRIN SCHACKE
↳205

STANLEY – THE OPEN QUESTION MAGAZINE

Self-initiated Work
Photo: Katrin Schacke

What does a black hole look like? And why don't our bodies simply continue to grow? Katrin Schacke has tackled such unresolved questions of humankind and discovered wonderfully imaginative images for them. As part of her thesis at the Academy of Art and Design Offenbach, she constructed an installation with inflated rubber gloves, bright orange plastic pools, and clouds of fog.

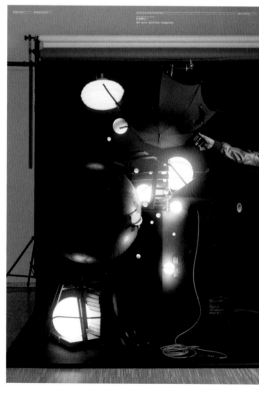

stanley ··
the open · question · magazine

HOW AND WHERE
DID LIFE ON
EARTH ARISE?

01 / 02 / 03 / **P96** 04 PARCOURS—
A GUIDE TOWARDS
SELF-EMPLOYMENT

Client: Transfer Center
Photo: Katrin Schacke

Young creative professionals know only too
well how laborious and challenging the path
to independence is. For beyond self-defined
works, each must also overcome legal and bu-
reaucratic hurdles. To ensure that »Parcours—
A Guide towards Self-employment« is a vivid
as well as informative read for the target group,
despite the dry enumeration of facts, Katrin
Schacke illustrates the individual chapters
with symbolic hurdles composed of the daily
utensils of the craft of a self-employed professional in the creative field.

01

02

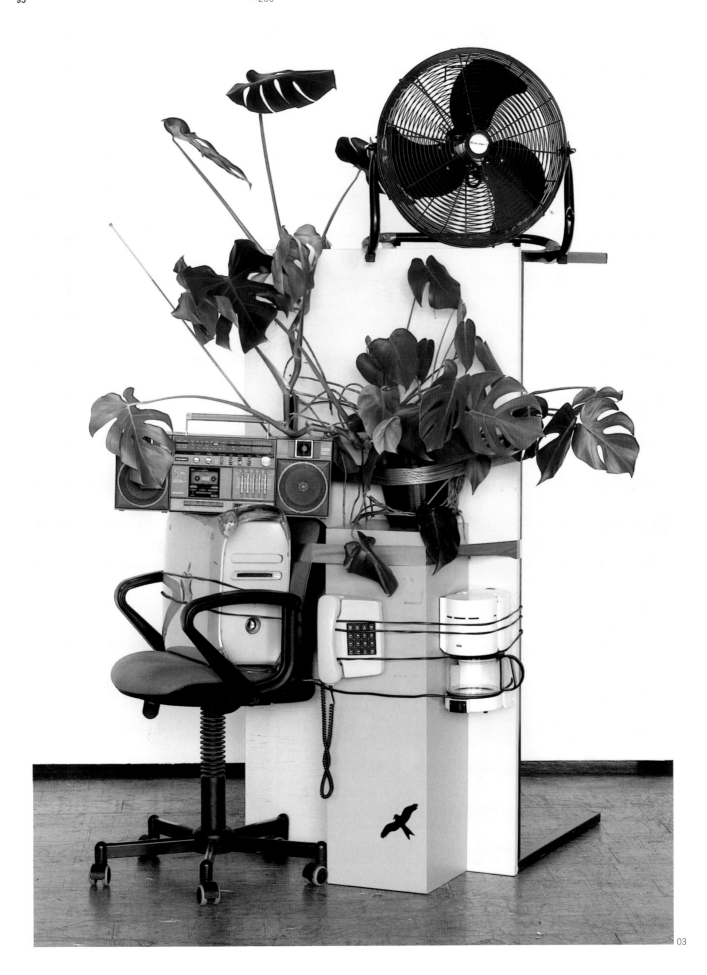

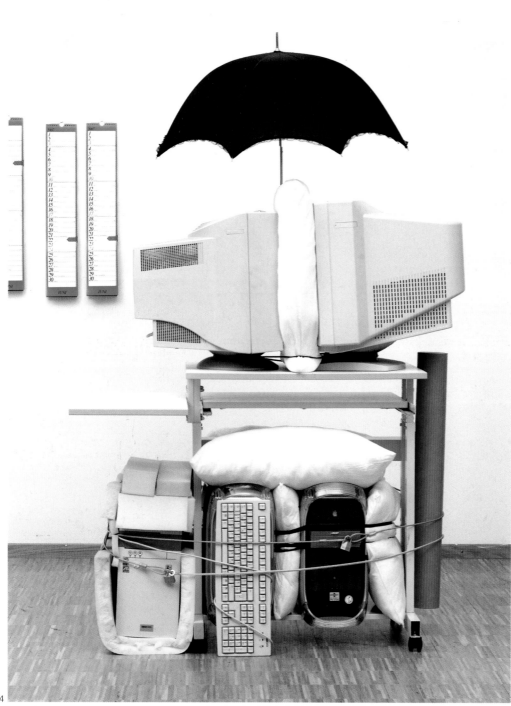

+41 //DIY
↳40→202

+41 COLLECTION 07

Client: +41

The name +41, a reference to the international telephone area code for Switzerland, stands for the fashion label of the Swiss graphic design label DIY. The designers work in the fields of fashion, music, illustration, art direction, and video. They present their new collection as a pile of clothes: jackets, pants, and sweatshirts are illustrated with simple graphic elements and form a gesture in the space.

01 NOT A GIRL NOT YET A WOMAN

Self-initiated Work

The installation »Not a girl not yet a woman«
is reminiscent of the experiments carried out
by the Memphis group that revolutionized
fashion design in the 1980s with their postmod-
ern formal language. Trivial and elementary
forms are combined into colorful and cheerful
collections of quotes. The large-format play
meadow was designed by the Danish design
team Hvass&Hannibal for an exhibition
held by the underground artists' collective
Artrebels in Copenhagen.

02

03

02/03/**P101** 05 TURBOWEEKEND

Client: Turboweekend
Photo: Hvass&Hannibal

Hvass&Hannibal's love of experimentation is also evident in the work for the Danish underground rock band »Turboweekend«. All physical objects in the space—including the band members—become carriers of color, with the result that graphic and plastic or 3-D spatial effects alternate in the composition as a whole.

HVASS&HANNIBAL
↳202

04 TURBOWEEKEND – NIGHTSHIFT

Client: Turboweekend / Copenhagen Records
Photo: Brian Buchard

For the album cover of the same band, Hvass&Hannibal stood on ladders behind the backdrop and tossed black-and-white confetti down onto the scene. The graphic particles, tumbling through the air and raining down gently on the band members, who were reclining on the floor, set the entire image in motion. In addition to the centralized perspective that is alluded to, the fragments of paper also create a sense of depth. In much the same way as in optical illusions, the image oscillates between a three-dimensional and a flat image, and it was precisely this effect that guided the deliberate digital processing that followed.

04

FUNK SINATRA
SEASON 3 & 4

Client: Funk Sinatra

What might appear like the setup for a photo shoot in the studio is in fact the outcome of a carefully composed installation of props. Mimetically reversible, both images are front and back cover, respectively, of one and the same double album, with the result that one actually holds two albums in one's hands, visually speaking. The props represent a universe of objects in the world of »Funk Sinatra«, and each of these objects is in turn referenced in the lyrics of the songs on the album.

PHILIPPE JARRIGEON

01

02

01/02 ERWIN

Self-initiated Work

The models aren't real people but personified objects, playing with the external image of male and female clichés. Long lashes on the spoiler of a sports car or layers of powder on the hood emphasize the humanoid features of the cars.

03 CAGOULES

Self-initiated Work

The young photoartist Philippe Jarrigeon also alters surfaces in his series titled »Cagoules«, or masks. In this case the alteration is applied to faces, which are covered in masks fashioned of handmade fabrics and citing as well as abstracting historic dress styles. Although equipped only with openings for the eyes, the draperies invest the heads with an expression all their own. Fabric patterns replace personal facial characteristics.

03

MANYSTUFF—VERY NICE

in collaboration with Nicolas Burrows
Client: Manystuff

In response to the question of what the significance of the interplay between digital and handmade design processes might be, Julien Vallée and Nicolas Burrows developed a computer screen that spills its contents onto a desk in a very real manner. The sterility that emanates from this spillage, despite its undisputed tactile qualities, corresponds to the digital esthetic of computer-generated images.

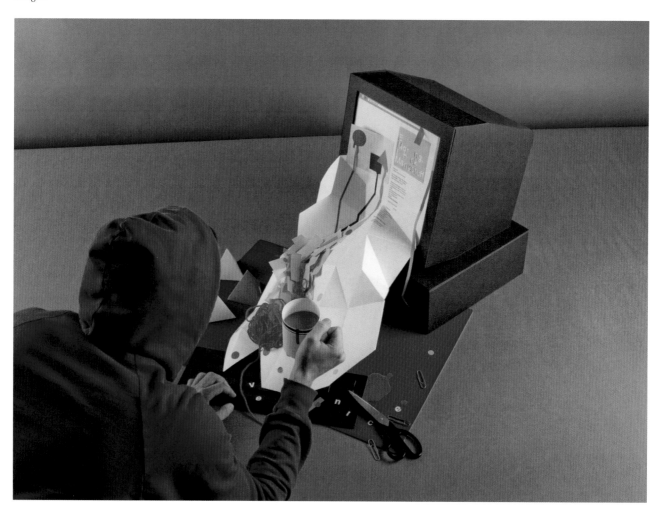

WITHOUT TITLE

Client: Das Magazin

Körner Union employ a simple trick to illustrate a scientific article on the topic of parallel worlds for the Swiss publication »Das Magazin«.

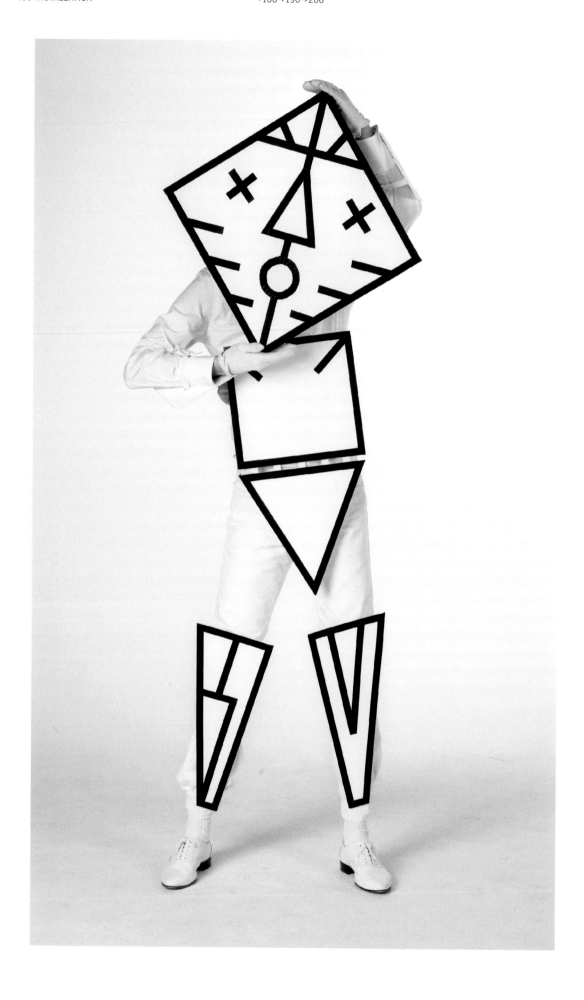

DOKTOR KOSMOS

Client: Doktor Kosmos

Swedengraphics transformed people into graphic figures for the cover of the album by Doktor Kosmos. Hidden behind geometrical masks and body fragments, the protagonists merge into the gleaming whiteness of the space, yielding the foreground to the graphic symbols.

HORT
↳46→178→198→203

R.M.B.

Client: R.M.B.

On the occasion of the tenth anniversary
of R.M.B., one of the most popular and
successful acts in the German techno scene,
Hort designed a variety of anniversary
motifs. Music, depicted in the form of vinyl
records and covers, appears to be succes-
sively seizing possession of human beings
and their environment.

HERE / NOW

Self-initiated Work
Photo: Thomas Balzer / Valerie Sietzy

Valerie Sietzy's installation »Here / Now«
is all about the moment. When light—be it
a camera flash or the lamp of a passing
bicycle—falls on the walls of the underpass,
the reflectors installed there form their
unexpected message. Barely perceptible
in daytime among the usual graffiti, nocturnal illumination unveils words and
drawings with which the graduate from
Offenbach's Academy of Art and Design
designed a total of 320 square meters
of a highway bridge.

PLAYAREA
↳180→205

POINTER KAMPAGNE

Client: Pointer Footwear

Playarea's concept for the shoe label Pointer consisted of creating robot-like yet individual figures, instead of models. The artists Marcus Oakley, Jo Ratcliffe, and Jethro Hynes were commissioned to create the sculptures. The soft shadows and the suggestion of three-dimensionality in these images emphasized the impression of real sculptures. The success of the first campaign was continued in two further variations, in which »real« people were ultimately included in the shots.

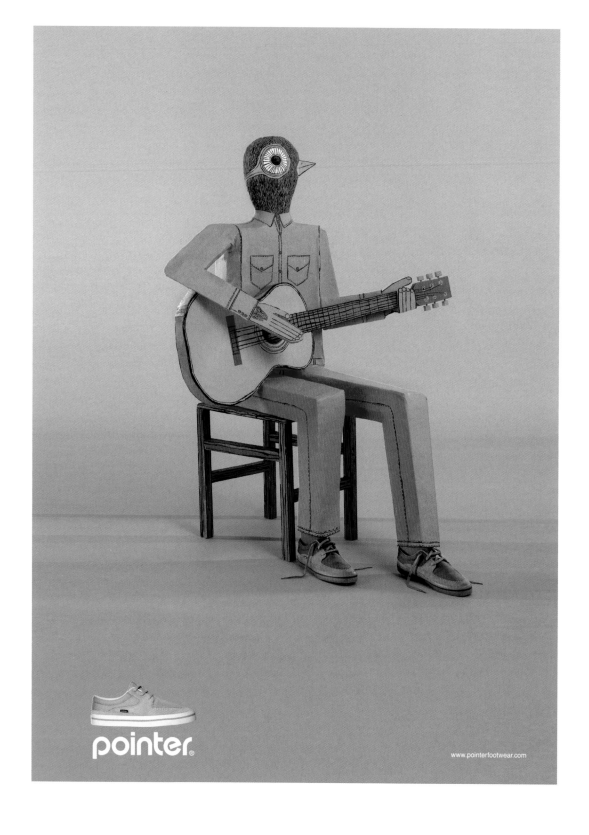

www.pointerfootwear.com

RITA'S LIVING ROOM

Self-initiated Work

The credo of the Canadian designers is manifest in »Rita's Living Room« according to which all types of design, regardless of medium and scale, can inspire each other and that just linking these types can lead to new formal and functional solutions. In their showroom, with printed crates that reflect an everyday mix of styles beyond chic lounge culture, the Rita group confronts the visitor with the question of the nature of design.

01

01 VW TRANSPORTER

Self-initiated Work

The VW Transporter installation consists of
an electrical cable, clamps, and a light bulb
with a socket. As a commentary on so-called
»socket [or: plug-in] art«, used in the artistic
jargon chiefly for media-based works that are
dependent on power, the works by the artist
from Graz, Austria, mix everyday themes and
low-fi electronics to create ironic arrangements.

02 NIKE AIR

Self-initiated Work

The everyday objects used by Valentin Ruhry
in his installations bring ready-mades to mind.
Upon closer inspection, however, we realize
that while these objects mimic their industri-
ally manufactured models, they have nevertheless been invested with remarkable characteristics by the artist.

02

MAGIC HANDS

Self-initiated Work

The magic hands, which cause scissors and
cotton balls to dance in the air, are based on
a principle that is as simple as it is sophisticated. When the designers of A Nice Idea Every
Day went to a DIY store, they had the idea of
photographing objects as seen through a sheet
of plexiglass, thus creating the impression of
freely floating materials.

FLYING THINGS

Self-initiated Work

A white plastic chair that materialized one fine morning in their rear courtyard inspired the design duo A Nice Idea Every Day to toss it into the air and take shots of the event. Because the flight characteristics of the chair turned out to be visually attractive, additional objects had to follow its example.

→

TOUCHING TYPE

IDON'TLIKEYOU, I'VENEVERLIKED-YOU: When Ben Freeman [→ p. 137] depicts sentences of this kind as razor blades, the directness of the depiction comes as a surprise. And yet it isn't the pictorial treatment of type that provokes a second look. After all, this is a popular exercise in every foundation course in typography and—at the very least since the advertising of the 1950s—an all too well-known principle. Therefore, what is astonishing in Freeman's work is that these are real razor blades. From the butcher's knife for coarse attacks to the stiletto for pointed invectives, the very shape of the knife is an indication of the attack that follows. Yet, instead of modifying the type in such a manner as to resemble the silhouette of razor blades—in true typographical tradition—the designer translates the idea into tangible weapons of action and has bronze blades cast in the form of type. As unmistakable and simple as the message may be for the viewer, the creation of the motif, from the carved cedar handle to the cast blade, is undoubtedly extremely elaborate. The effort invested in this independent work inspires curiosity: is the focus on trying out unusual design elements? Or is it all about the principle of reversing pictorial typography into legible images?

When Pleaseletmedesign [→ p. 169] pins the wording of a poster for the Court Circuit association—composed of electrical wires—on a wall, the result is a chaotic assemblage of cables, image and type all in one. Works like these are no doubt provocative to proponents of a rational and functional use of typography. Statements of principle for designing with type, according to which clarity, order, and precision represent the maxims of good design in the sense of legibility, are widely familiar. Isn't type regarded as particularly fitting when it isn't even noticed? Or do the well-known quotes by giants of typography such as Adrian Frutiger or Kurt Weidemann simply refer to reading typology?

The demand for a type selection that can communicate content in such a way that the message is immediately understood may still offer at least some room for play: unless the primary purpose is to convey purely informative content—user instructions, for example, or product information pamphlets in packaging—idiosyncratic typology can be perfectly functional. Hence the basic question is related to purpose. Even the aforementioned banners from the 1950s fulfilled their advertising function precisely because they captured the attention of consumers with noticeable, catchy compositions. And when Elisabeth Moch [→ p. 157] assembles the confessional statement »Nobody knows me« from crumbs of dried autumn leaves, there is no doubt that type on its own could never convey the melancholy nature of this message with similar precision.

Good typography responds to the specific context and limiting it to objectivity, anonymity, and functionality would undoubtedly cause it to fall short of its true potential. The workshops of the Dutch collective Underware [→ p. 172] illustrate just how unconventional context and type can be. In the search for suitable building blocks for type, books, shopping carts, or toilet paper rolls are used. The results show to what degree the choice of a relevant material influences the impact of the words. The

message »Dream on«, composed of arranged shopping carts on a supermarket parking lot, would surely invoke different associations if it were formed of books or briefcases.

If one looks at the collected works in this volume from the perspective of objectivity, that term clearly takes on a highly unusual significance. For type becomes object in the real sense. Be it sewn by hand, as in Elene Usdin's photographs, woven from plastic bands by Catrin Sonnabend [→ p. 132], or composed of letter-shaped candles by Jennie Hancock—neither material nor effort are spared to give words dimension in the literal sense. The results of this approach to working with typography tap into artistic and creative precepts of Concrete Art and Poetry, all the while evading classification of any kind. The designers represented here expand the resources of visual communication, adding a plethora of new materials and methods. When three-dimensional space replaces the two-dimensional surface—as is the case in the works of Pleaseletmedesign [→ p. 170], Kong [→ p. 158], or Eike König's Hort (lit. »Refuge«) [→ S.178]—the usual grids are replaced by scenic qualities. These effects, employing simple means that range from taping over irrelevant spaces to type composed of paper in different colors, are as simple as they are impactful. In this context, it is worth drawing special attention to the poster design for Effenaar, for the perspective rendered in the background of the image is no more than a lined cardboard box, albeit not recognizable as such by the observer. On the folded, two-dimensional

paper surfaces, cutout banners, light, and shadow combine to create a fascinating depth of space.

Other works employ the shift between three-dimensionality and two-dimensional area in a collage of text composed of a wide range of objects. When seen from the relevant perspective, tools and materials convey a Christmas greeting, while a seemingly chaotic collection of watches sends out a message at just the right moment when all the minute and hour hands are synchronized to form the relevant message. In addition to experiments with dimensionality and perception, other, entirely unexpected, techniques are also incorporated into the practice of design. The sewn and wood-crafted letters by Swedengraphics [→ p. 166], or the handwritten scripts carved from model foam for the Wordwide project, round out the repertoire of the disciplines.

The German word »Kunsthandwerk« (crafts, literally handcrafted art) elicits nothing but irritation among designers; at the Nova Scotia College of Art and Design in Halifax, Canada, on the other hand, a new term was created for the English language: »Neocraft«. Neocraft describes the mix of craft, art, and design employed here, the origins of which date back to the British Arts and Crafts Movement and the Wiener Werkstätten. In other words, to design movements whose ideas were as revolutionary in their day as they were influential in the subsequent development of the relevant disciplines. As design gained in significance and industrial mass production began to take over the world, the appreciation for handcrafted design decreased during the second half of the twentieth century.

Given that the handmade, decorative, and yet original qualities of working with a craft are being revived by designers, of all people, one must ask what lies behind such an about-face. The rejection of established design practices suggests causes that surely go beyond purely formal-esthetic phenomena.

Until now, customizing—the potential variability in how individual parts are combined—was regarded as an alternative to the standardized industrial product. From custom-configured running shoes to individualized car interiors, mass-customization opened the door to affordable products that suit individual needs and tastes.

Ultimately, consumers have digitalization to thank for the linkage of industrial manufacture and individual stylistic preferences, as user-friendly programs make it possible to design products on a computer. It is interesting to note that most of these applications provide consumers with style templates. The client can then choose among such so-called »designs« or freely combine individual elements. However, when design becomes a style template, then every amateur becomes a designer. And when production technological perfection becomes a matter of course, then any deviation from the norm gains in significance. When applied to the examples gathered here, this paradigm shift may go some way toward explaining the multiplicity of individual work traces. Loosely scattered material remnants appear like haphazard proof of the handmade creation of the motif.

Room corners and architectural details convey a workshop character and offer a staged glance into the work process. In this return to so-called handcrafted methods, the focus isn't on the usual high-gloss esthetic. Instead, the purpose is to render originality visible.

It is hardly surprising, therefore, that designers everywhere are profiling themselves as part of the scenery or, at least, integrating real people into their image worlds. Thus individual body parts, as well as entire groups of bodies, are incorporated into the design. Superficially employed as a functional element, for example as the down stroke in a letter, the human body within the pictorial world serves as an ultimate guarantor of scale and dimension. Where the human form as scale is not included, there are at least human traces as a mark of authenticity. Small irregularities emphasize a deliberate renunciation of image editing and processing. We can only guess how much staging is in fact invested in precisely these incidental details.

Text: Sophia Muckle

01 CORPS TYPOGRAPHIQUE

Self-initiated Work

In »Corps Typografique« (»Body Type«), Benoit Lemoine illustrated the idea of the formal analogy between the human body and the corporeal nature of letters. The work is an attempt to document this relationship in a kind of lexicon. Each typographical theme is represented by a poster that enhances the similarities by photographic means. The circumference or measurement of the (human) body corresponds to individual letters. Thus the French word g.r.a.i.s.s.e.—which means »bold« as a type or font attribute in English— is a pictorial rendering of the letters with the help of layers of clothing.

02 PRÉPA ÉCOLES D'ART

Client: Beaux-Arts de Saint-Brieuc (France)

In France, attending preparatory classes is the norm prior to taking entrance exams for schools of higher learning (universities, schools of art and architecture, etc.). The motif for the graduation exhibition of works created during these classes has been realized by the team Repeatafterme in the form of layered sheets of colored paper on the wall and floor. The pattern on the floor is intended as an abstract geographic site plan of the school, while the paper layers on the wall represent the continual exercises and repetitions that will characterize the studies of these future students.

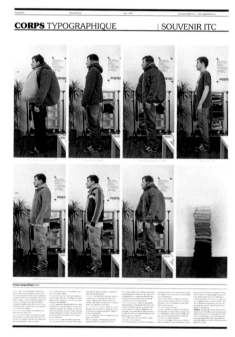

01

Classe préparatoire
aux examens d'entrée
des écoles d'art,
des mises à niveau
d'arts appliqués,
des écoles d'architecture.

Ecole municipale
des Beaux-Arts
Centre Charner
22000 Saint-Brieuc

Téléphone : 0299625521
Fax : 0296943715
beaux-arts3@wanadoo.fr
www.prepa-art-bretagne.fr

Saint-Brieuc
NOTRE QUALITÉ DE VILLE

ART DIRECTORS CLUB YOUNG GUNS 5 LIVE IDENTITY PACKAGE

Client: Art Directors Club, NYC
Art Direction: Jennifer Lew, WSDIA
Photo: Mastromatteo + Steen

Are the invitations to the Young Guns Live Event legible images or staged typography? Young Guns Live is a series of events running parallel to the competition of the same name held by the Art Directors' Club of New York. Old and new Young Guns award winners gathered on the podium for the four themes of the competition: »The Woman Vanguard«, »Big/Small«, »DIY« and »Frame by Frame«. In collaboration with the design office WSDIA from Brooklyn, designer Jennifer Lew created posters and invitations for these events.

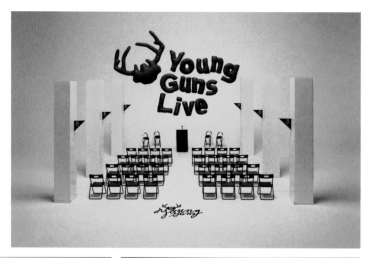

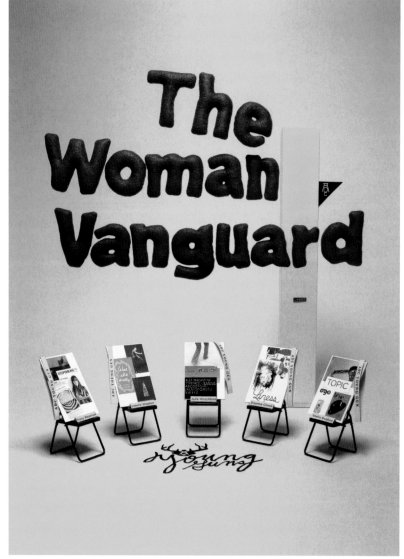

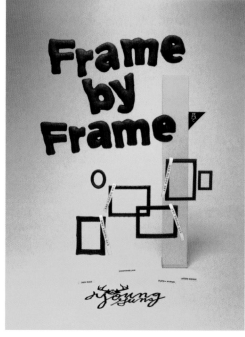

LARK MAGAZINE PHOTO SHOOT

Client: Lark magazine
Photo: Tim Brown

Sometimes simply playing around with
objects is sufficient to tap into new ideas.
»Lark« magazine has chosen this approach as
a principle, and elevates ordinary objects
to become catalysts for creative exploration.
In their contributions, participating designers
explore overlooked qualities or neglected
topics. A metal ruler inspired Tim Brown to
create the works featured here, prompting
him to show tiny objects on a vastly increased
scale.

BACKBREAKER TYPE

Client: Project for Patrick Coppens,
Gerrit Rietveld Academy, Amsterdam
Photo: Monica Tormell, Tomas Adolfs
Modelle: Kalle Mattsson, Britta Persson

An old woodcut type, in which the letters
were formed from human figures, inspired
Kalle Mattsson to create his Backbreaker
type. Since the historical model used a sail to
create the letter P, the typographic remake
also incorporated a playful take on wind and
weather. Kalle Mattsson chose the windiest
location in his surroundings as a site and set
to work in the company of his friends. Backbreaker type takes its name from the body
position assumed to form the letter C.

FESTIVAL JUNGER TALENTE

Client: Verein für Kulturförderung Rhein-Main e. V.
Art Direction: Catrin Sonnabend and Christina Föllmer

The »Festival of Young Talents« is an art exhibition held in Offenbach, Germany, and organized every two years by the four art schools in the state of Hessen. The aim of the festival is to promote collaboration among students in the fields of art, music, dance, and film. With the goal of visually translating the link-age of different disciplines, designers Catrin Sonnabend and Christina Föllmer turned to materials found in the context of a construction site. In addition to the poster motif, the invitations, and the exhibition catalogue, they also employed the materials for the signage and orientation system through the exhibition.

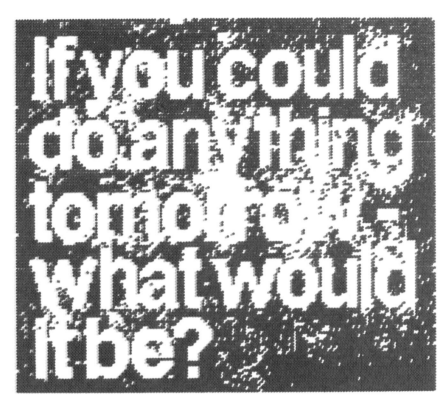

IF YOU COULD COVER

in collaboration with Will Hudson and Ian Wright
Client: If You Could magazine

With the challenge »If you could do anything tomorrow—what would it be?« designers Alex Bec and Will Hudson initiated a competition for artists and designers, whose works explore the very same query. The eponymous and long since sold out magazine published 112 responses. More than 10,000 Hama beads were required for the cover design.

ALEX BEC
↳201

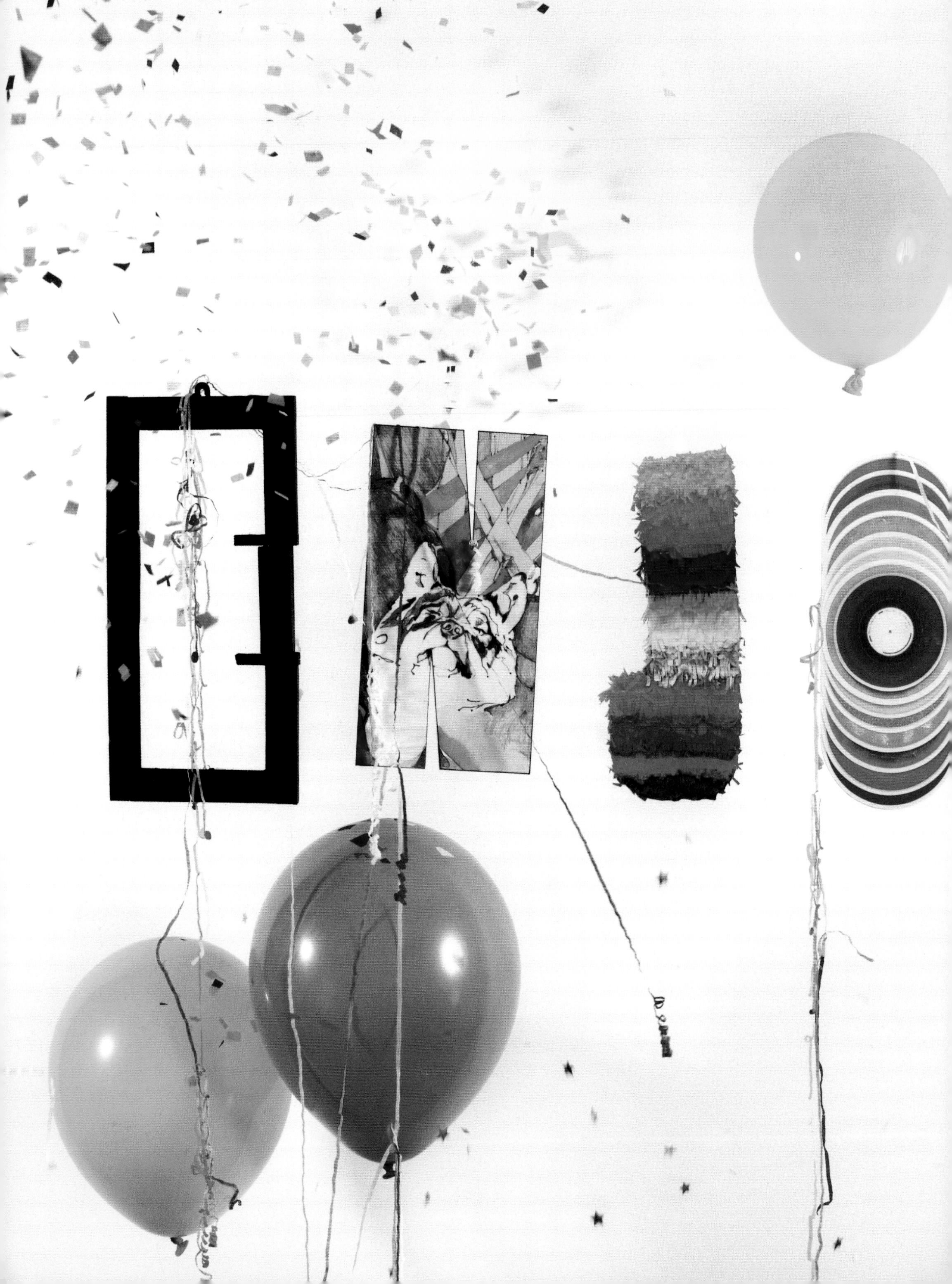

YCN ALPHABET

Client: YCN / Young Creative Network, London
Art Direction: Alex Bec, Michael Bojkowski
Photo: Anni Collinge

Through launching annual competitions and
events, YCN provides a platform for designers
and also serves as a bridge between training
and practice. For the YCN yearbook, Alex
Bec charged young designers with the task
of designing a single letter each. The images
created with these letters were then used as
divider pages in the publication's inside.

01 TOUCH TYPE

Self-initiated Work / Royal College of Art

How does one's own perception change a typeface when its letters have to be discerned through the sense of touch? Ben Freeman transferred a playful experiment on his partner's back to the typeface for a ceramics exhibition: a letter was written on the back of each exhibitor, who was then in turn invited to draw the form of the letter, based on tactile perception, into a bed of clay. The designer then transformed the impressions into a positive by creating plaster casts, which were then digitized and utilized as the typeface for the exhibition.

02 VICIOUS STATEMENTS

Self-initiated Work

Ben Freeman carved three-dimensional letters in wax representing the most hurtful words his friends could remember ever having been shouted at them. He then cast the wax maquettes in bronze. To finalize the pieces, the bronze pieces had to be polished and equipped with handcarved and sanded cedar handles. In the designer's own words, the scent of the materials themselves, in addition to the appeal of working in a hands-on manner, was a quality that the usual (design) work on a computer simply cannot offer.

02

THE PATH TO THE
CORRECT TYPE

Client: Page magazine
Art Direction and Design: Mario Lombardo
Graphic Design: Mirjana Parovic

Many a designer may despair over the sheer
endless selection of fonts and type that has
become a matter of course in the age of digital
design processes. Clear ideas and decisions
are needed to find a path out of this maze of
randomness. Mario Lombardo visualizes the
decision process as a life-size labyrinth—in
reality, a mere 15 cm in height.

→

»I HAD TO EVOLVE BACKWARD«
Interview with Mario Lombardo

Photo: Michael Mann

Mr. Lombardo, from 2001 to 2006 you were the art director of the German music magazine »Spex«. Since 2004 you have also been working independently as Bureau Mario Lombardo. From the outset you developed a strikingly analogous visual language in »Spex«, for example, with collages of images or photographs sewn together. Was that a conscious break with the usual computer esthetic?
You probably can't call it a conscious break. It was more that »Spex« had to get by on a minimal budget, and so I did most of the design myself. Because I never much liked designing on the computer, that way of working came about very gradually and developed from task to task, as it were.

How are we to imagine that? Did you simply start at some point arranging things in space and photographing them?
It started out with collages, but then at some point they no longer offered enough room to play—or more precisely, they spread out in space. Design expanded, so to speak, and incorporated materials and spaces in the process. For that reason, there is still a connection between my works and the place where they were created. And this way of working is also in keeping with my view that graphic art should have something human about it. After all, the point is to communicate with people.

Does a striving for authenticity play a role in that?
I think it's primarily about emotionality, about moods that I can convey more directly by working this way. That don't have to be reconstructed but are already present in the work, in the material used and the space chosen.

And that isn't possible on a computer?
When I was studying in the 1990s, computer work was evolving rapidly. The effects of David Carson were still in the air, and of course everyone was designing using computers. But I never really enjoyed that sort of work. I had to evolve backward, so to speak. But I was and still am sure: genuine materials have a totally different directness.

For example?
For the fashion issues of »Spex«, I had come up with a concept that could then evolve over the years. To do that, I first looked around at fashion and then decided to use the seam as a design element for the first issue, the cut for the second, and materiality for the third. For the first edition, I borrowed a sewing machine from my sister and sewed parts of pictures together. Naturally they had to be scanned afterward, and for that I used a computer again. When sewing I could react spontaneously and ultimately arrive at a finished design much more quickly than if I had simulated the seams in Photoshop. And time always played an important role in the monthly issues of »Spex«.

Was your approach subject to criticism at the time?
Yes, people kept telling me the design lacked continuity. But in fact the continuity consisted precisely of constantly refining the concept.

Where do you find inspiration for your ideas today?
I take walks. I get lots of ideas when I'm out and about. The idea for the cover of the anniversary compilation for Background Records, for example, came to me when I was at the zoo with my nephew, and we were standing, fascinated, in front of the aquariums with the jellyfish. Otherwise, my surroundings have always provided me with stimuli. At my old office in Cologne, it was the neighboring buildings from the 1950s, and the unused clothesline in the courtyard, that we liked to use as a visual element. And the linoleum floor of the Cologne office was also very appealing. Recently we moved to Berlin, and now it's fascinating to see the effect the new environment has on our work. The new floor still makes me wonder ... A classic parquet floor simply has a different aura than linoleum—it might send the wrong signal ...

Interview: Sophia Muckle

01

01 BACKGROUND RECORDS

Client: Background Records
Art Direction: Mario Lombardo
Design: Enver Hadzijaj and Mario Lombardo
Photo: Alfred Jansen

On the occasion of the seventh anniversary and the fiftieth album release by the minimal electronic label Background Records, Mario Lombardo transformed the basement of the Cologne studio into an imaginary aquarium populated by jellyfish and other sea creatures made of paper.

02 DIGITAL IS BETTER

Client: Spex magazine
Art Direction: Mario Lombardo
Design: Mario Koell
Photo: Alfred Jansen

Recording tape becomes typography: in this work Mario Lombardo cites the title of Tocotronic's debut album, »Digital ist besser«, released in 1995, in apparent contradiction to his own design style.

02

03/04 ANDY VAZ REMIXES

Client: persistencebit records
Art Direction: Mario Lombardo
Design: Mirjana Parovic, Mario Lombardo

Ficus Benjamini remixed: to ensure that the type on the album cover is also legible from a distance, the foliage of this indoor plant has to be rearranged. The arrangement, in a rear courtyard in Cologne, demonstrates that Mario Lombardo's works often incorporate the design environment.

03

04

WAYS OF SEEING

Self-initiated Work

With the help of typographical elements, Jennie Hancock explores what happens when type is liberated from the digital context. »Ways of Seeing« tests legibility and perception in different spatial scenes.

JOCELYN COTTENCIN
↳202

OXYGEN CONSUMPTION
DIFFERS FROM ONE
INDIVIDUAL TO THE NEXT

Self-initiated Work

The script »La Consommation d'oxygène est
différente d'un individu à l'autre«, composed
of floral patterns, was originally designed by
artist and graphic designer Jocelyn Cottencin
for a solo exhibition. When he subsequently
decided to transfer the work to a public space,
the artist looked for a material that would
adapt to the context of the street. Convinced
that the phrase would soon disappear from
wall surfaces usually utilized for advertising
and graffiti alike, he used chalk to draw the
floral patterns, with the help of a group of art
students. Surprisingly, the work, a comment on
the oxygen consumed by each human being,
remained intact for three years.

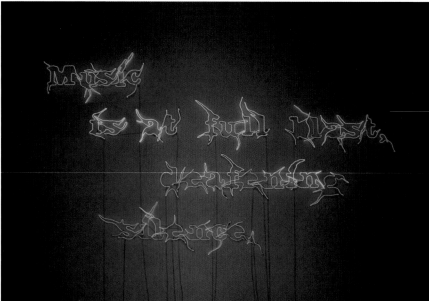

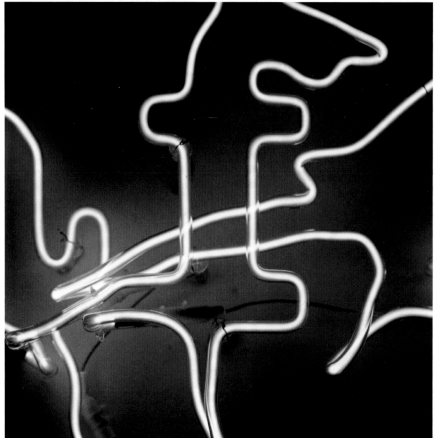

MUSIC AT FULL BLAST IS DEAFENING SILENCE

Self-initiated Work

In his works, French artist and graphic designer Jocelyn Cottencin combines typography, pictorial moments, and aspects of space and movement. The banner »Music At Full Blast Is Deafening Silence«, composed of fluorescent tubes, was created within the context of the project »Just a Walk«, initiated by Cottencin, in which various artists collaborated to explore the sociogeographical changes along the western borders of Europe.

FLORIAN JENETT
↳203

DON'T TELL ANYBODY

Self-initiated Work

Calm reigns for just a brief moment when the
accumulation of lines forms a legible sentence.
Yet the passage of time, which we are reminded
of by the clock hands, causes the message to
disintegrate into a chaotic stream of symbols.
A full twelve hours must pass before the fragments once again form a legible meaning, for a
brief sixty seconds.

01 BYGGBOOKS

Self-initiated Work
Photo: Byggstudio

With a playful and unconventional design
approach, Byggstudio from Denmark moves
between illustration, graphic design, and set
design. The minimal arrangement composed
of the elements book, man, and space, densi-
fies several design fields in a single image.
Incidentally, the books that were used to
compose the word »BYGG« were borrowed
from the local public library.

02 FASHION DJ'S

Client: Soundvenue Fashion Issues
Photo: Andreas Larsson

The names Jean and Kjeld refer to the Danish
music scene DJs Jean von Baden and Kjeld
Tholdstrup. Since the fan communities of these
artists are distinct from one another even in
their dress style, Byggstudio conceived the
idea of utilizing the fashionable accessories
from their respective scenes to create the type
for the two names.

02

01 GRRRRR PANG! ZZZZZ

Client: Dazed & Confused and Wrangler

Damien Poulain's wooden text blocks were inspired by the onomatopoeic exclamations that are typical of comics. Freed from the narrative content of a comic-book story, the handpainted crates become images in their own right. The text blocks were created for the Wrangler »Wanted« tour in 2007 through the European cities of Barcelona, Stockholm, and Milan.

02 AN UGLY GIRL BLAMES THE MIRROR

Client: Blanka
Photo: Tara Darby

The verb »provoke« was the initial inspiration for the work »An Ugly Girl Blames the Mirror« by Damien Poulain. As one of twenty-eight designers, he was asked on the occasion of the London Design Festival to pick one word from a list of twenty-eight and to interpret it. With his contribution, Damien Poulain demonstrates the communicative power of images.

01

An

UGLY

girl

BLAMES

the

.Mirror

KOKON TO ZAI

Client: Kokon To Zai, London

Since their collaboration with the fashion
label began in 2004, Eat Sleep Work/Play have
developed a unique pictorial vocabulary
for communications related to the shops in
London and Paris. From online presence to
lookbooks for their own KTZ line, they have
employed bright colors, analog interpretations,
and sophisticated visual effects—all corre-
sponding to the fashion. For the tenth anniversary of the label, Eat Sleep Work/Play
produced visuals that were assembled live
during the anniversary party and projected.

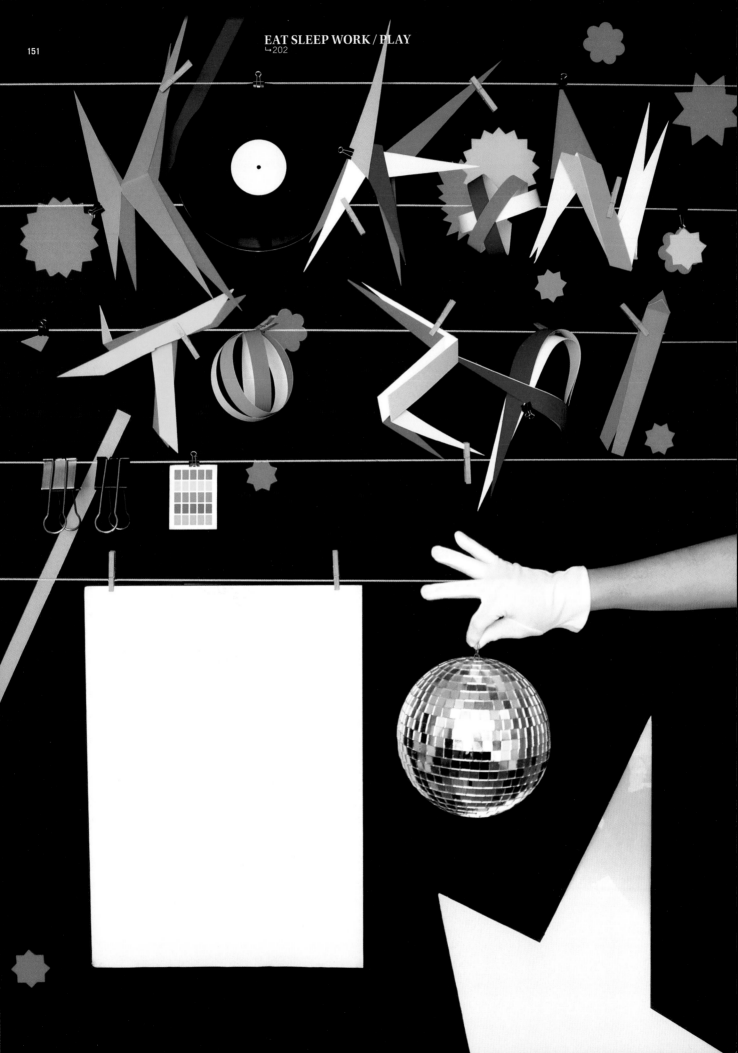

MODULAR

Client: Modular

For the weekly club nights of London-based record label Modular, Eat Sleep Work/Play created visuals and invitations. To translate the name of the label in graphics, in accordance with the building-block principle, the designers fabricated the individual letters and photographed them against a backdrop of colored paper strips.

ALRT

Client: Effenaar
Concept and Design: EDHV, Remco van de Craats
and Eric de Haas

The design concept for the flyers and posters announcing the first series of ALRT events in the Dutch town of Eindhoven was based on the idea of developing a pictorial language that would be as analog as possible. Thus the spatial staging of type was realized in a lined moving box. The dramatic effect of swaths of color and shadow was achieved entirely by means of a hole in the bottom of the box through which a bright light shines into the interior.

WORDWIDE

Self-initiated Work
Art Direction: Remco van de Craats
Design: Sjoerd Koopmans, Remco van de Craats

What would happen if you sent a famous quote on a journey, word by word, and asked the recipients for a photograph in return? For the »Wordwide« experiment, the designers of EDHV took handwritten words of the media theoretician Marshall McLuhan and had them jet-streamed out of modeling foam. Packed in small boxes, the words were then sent to designers throughout the world with a request to stage their own context for the specific word they received. Marshall McLuhan, renowned for his thesis that »the medium is the message« would likely have appreciated the altered effect of his original statement.

NEW KIDS ON THE BLOG

Self-initiated Work

The blog entries of three teenagers served as inspiration for Elisabeth Moch's thesis work at the Design College of Düsseldorf. Without ever establishing direct contact with the teens, the designer followed their everyday and personal blogs and messages on the Internet over a period of six months. Moch then designed a book with material culled from the blog entries: »Actually I started out wanting to do my homework« (this page) or »Somewhat bored« (opposite page).

JOYEUSES FÊTES ...

Self-initiated Work

New camera equipment inspired the designers at the Swiss design studio Kong to use photography for their Christmas and New Year's cards. New Year's resolutions and the usual hectic activity that surrounds Christmas are reflected in the mountains of material and paper on the desks.

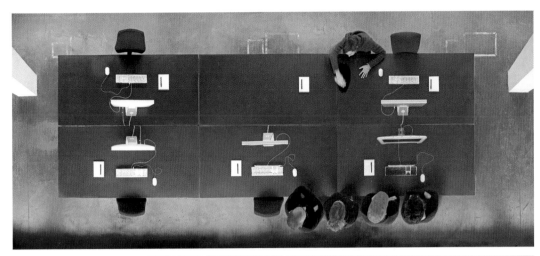

SUPER DESIGN MARKET

Client: London Design Festival

The second »Super Design Market« was held in the Royal Festival Hall as part of the London Design Festival. Over thirty product designers were selected for the event and given the opportunity to sell their work direct to the public. Multistorey collaborated with the exhibition designer Mark Garisde to develop and create the graphic elements for the event. Since the huge open space was host to several events at the same time, the team sought to find a solution that would be visible from all angles and sightlines without competing with the adjacent exhibitions. Hundreds of meters of fabric in the corporate colors of the event were wrapped and knotted around the concrete pillars that support the roof of the hall in order to create a canopy above the design market.

REBECCA STEPHANY
↳206

↳206

01 PARADISE IS MADE OF PAPER

Client: Gerrit Rietveld Academy, Amsterdam

02 FANFOLD

Self-initiated Work

The title of the work provides the clue: for Rebecca Stephany's works, paper is not merely a material that the design appears upon, it is the inspiration for the design. For the installation titled »Paradise Is Made Of Paper«, the graduate of the Gerrit Rietveld Academy floated paper letters like ideas above the heads of library visitors. When light is added to the installation, as simulated in the model for the roof slogan »Here«, the shadow that is cast creates a double image of the type.

02

⁰¹ **DISCO DRIVE—THINGS
TO DO TODAY CD**

Client: Unhip Records

In designing the cover for the album of the
Italian band Disco Drive, the designers of
Nous Vous were inspired by the album title
»Things To Do Today«. For the cover and
the accompanying booklet they used the
idiosynchratic esthetic of handwritten to-do
lists. The individual motifs for the cover were
constructed, arranged, and photographed
on a single day.

⁰² **MAN ALIVE POSTER**

Client: Man Alive Music and Art Event

Originally the site for the Man Alive events
was to be decorated in the way that is illustrated in miniature on the poster. Due to time
constraints in mounting such an elaborate
scene, and because a campfire complete with
tent and northern fire may well have caused
some problems with the site owner, the cardboard model had to suffice as decoration.

01

01/**P168** 02 ODDJOB

Client: Oddjob

Ever since the early 1960s and the legendary graphics by Reid Miles, jazz album cover design with expressive type has become associated with the image of Blue Note Records. Swedengraphics' designs for the jazz quintet Oddjob revive this tradition and take the Blue Note esthetic into the third dimension. The cover and poster design, realized with handsewn and woodcrafted letters, is as elaborate as it is unusual. For the second album, »Koyo«, the workshop atmosphere of the shooting is incorporated into the image, which can be interpreted as an analogy of musical and design working processes.

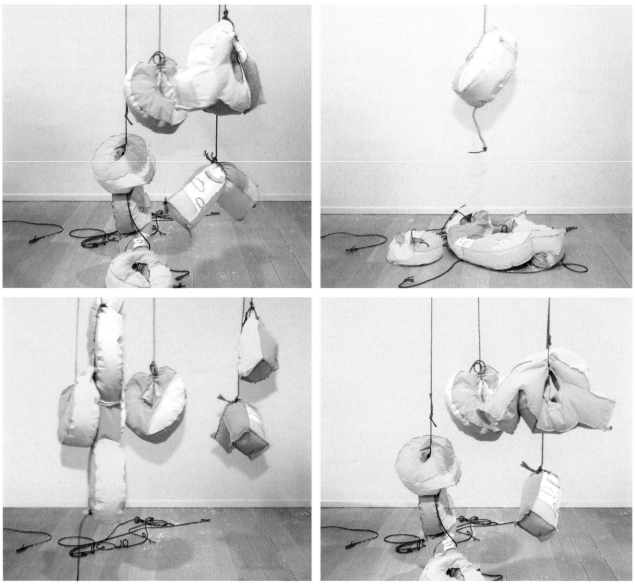

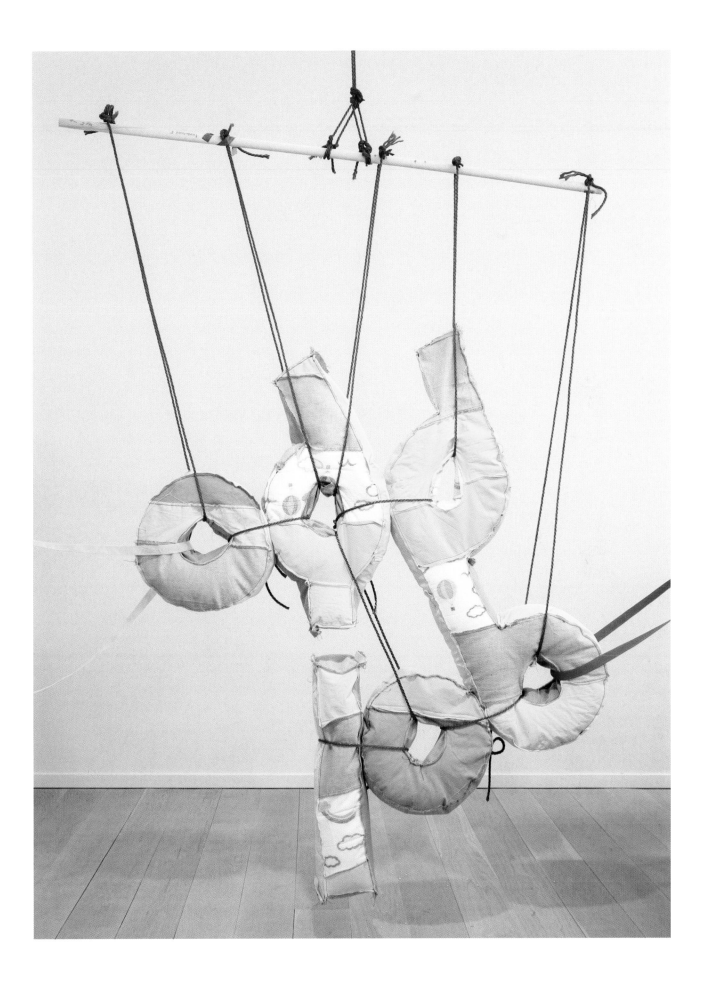

COURT-CIRCUIT

Client: Court-Circuit asbl

Court-Circuit is a Belgian organization dedicated to promoting young rock musicians in and from Belgium. Musicians are promoted through competitions, concerts, and CDs released under the organization's own label. Because the name Court-Circuit means »short circuit«, Pleaseletmedesign chose electrical cables as their design material. The various activities of the organization are represented by six thin electrical wires.

THE EXPERIMENTAL
TROPIC BLUES BAND

Client: The Experimental Tropic Blues Band

Pleaseletmedesign wanted to create a truly
big poster for »The Experimental Tropic Blues
Band«. The designers had already transferred
the lettering of the band name onto a scale
of 6 by 2.5 meters, and this scale was to be sur-
passed for this project. Since the musicians
of the psychobilly-punk-blues band are known
to enjoy whisky, the designers chose Scotch
tape as their design medium.

The Experimental
Tropic Blues Band

1. Rene The Renegade
2. Jealous Rock
3. Rising From The Dead
4. The Gambler
5. Twice Blues
6. Voodoo Rise
7. Gangrene Blues
8. Garbage Man
9. Snake VS Wolf
10. Dry Whiskey
11. Hallelujah
12. Mexico Dream Blues
13. I Went Down
14. Evil Can't Be Done

TYPEWORKSHOPS

A typographic cloak-and-dagger action which
could not have been realized without the necessary pocket change: in the context of a »type
workshop« organized by the Dutch design
studio Underware, young designers staged the
words »Dream on« on a supermarket parking
lot in Lausanne by arranging shopping carts
to spell out the letters. Even plain old bath-
room tissue or tape can become a typographic
message when employed in the appropriate
manner.

01 CNDC 2007−2008

02 LE GRAND DEHORS

Client: Contemporary Dance Center, Angers

For the launch of the season at the Contemporary Dance Center in the French town of Angers, the Paris design duo Antoine et Manuel created an entire ensemble of expressive figures, symbols, and letters, which are set in motion for the poster and for the booklet titled »le grand dehors«. Against the two-dimensional backdrop, it seems as if the twirling elements pause briefly in their choreography in order to convey their message to the viewer.

01

LE GRAND DEHORS

EMMANUELLE HUYNH

01 TRISHA BROWN
DANCE COMPANY
02 VIDEODANSE

Client: Contemporary Dance Center, Angers

The organic appearance of the typography for
the series of posters for the Contemporary
Dance Center seems to harmonize with the
dancers' limbs. The digitally created background enhances the spatial impact of type
and bodies, striving to free themselves from
props like actors on a stage.

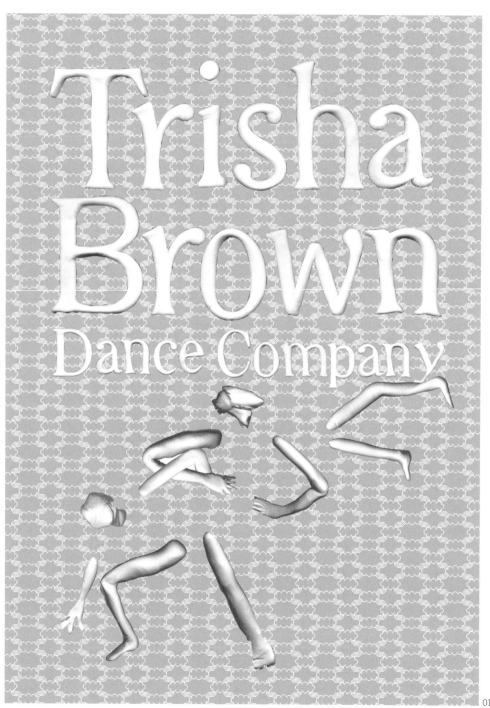

01

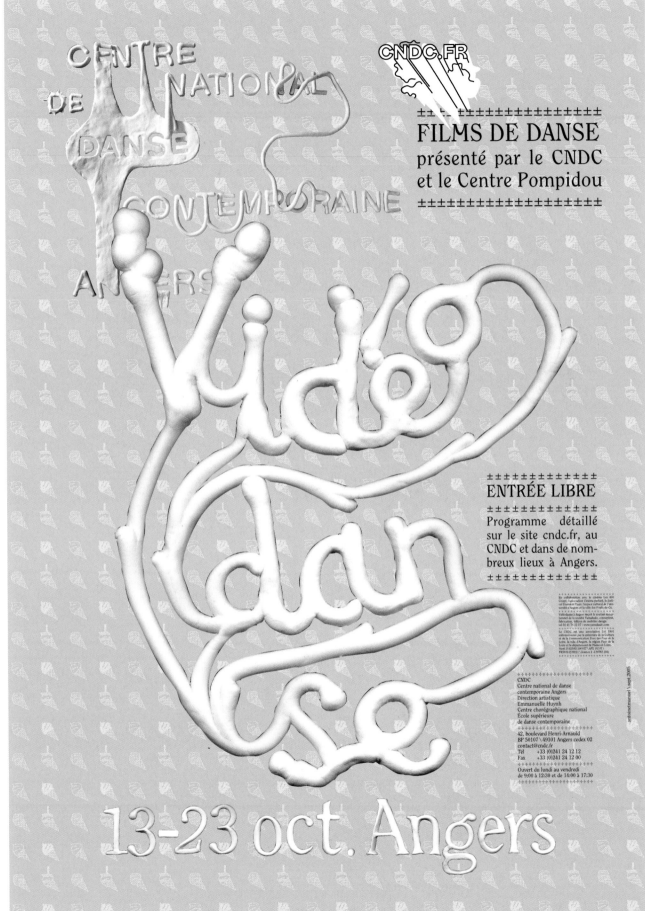

DJ KICKS

Client: Booka Shade

When Walter Merziger and Arno Kammermeier appear in public as Booka Shade, Eike König's Hort takes care of all aspects of the visual image for the producer team, from cover design to live visuals. Although the show of the two clay figures on the first cover design for »DJ Kicks« was rejected by Booka Shade, the clay backdrop created on the same occasion is being presented to the public after all.

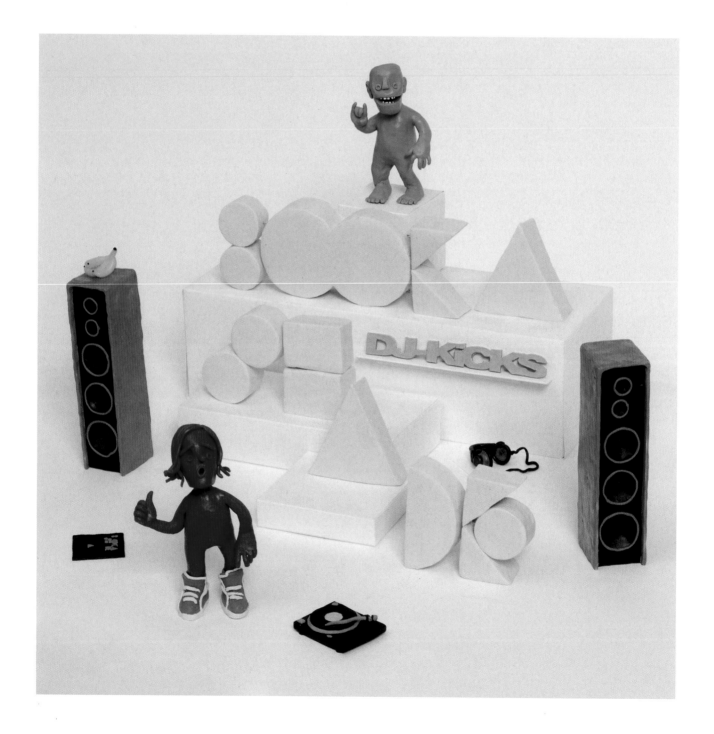

TIME TO SHINE

Client: Nike

When basketball players are able to fly, it is thanks to their footwear—at least that is what the advertisers say. In keeping with the motto for the Nike Summer Hoops program, the poster design for the Nike Art poster glows in airy white. While the spatial boundaries are blurred in the atmospheric background, the typography composed of constructed individual letters appears ready to take off and float out of the poster space, along with the basketball shoes, at any moment.

POINTER

Client: Pointer Footwear

With their letters composed according to the block system, Playarea illustrate what lies behind the label Pointer. Each letter becomes a display window showcasing the individual shoe models, organized into colorful thematic environments. The public image of the shoe label Pointer is defined by Playarea's design, from logo to color and fabric patterns all the way to packaging.

MCAD SPRING EVENTS CALENDAR

Client: Minneapolis College of Art and Design

Ryan Nelson and Vance Wellenstein have taken the practice of hanging a calendar on the wall in order to keep track of deadlines and schedules and applied it to their poster design for the Minneapolis College of Art and Design. Instead of schedule entries, the two alumni of the university selected visual placeholders for each event.

MCAD Events, Lectures & Exhibitions

→

THRILLING ANIMATIONS

When the 3-D scenarios of the preceding chapters are set into motion, the world of inanimate objects seems to come alive, launching into a life of its own as soon as we turn our backs. The fantastical events that befall objects when they »feel unobserved« are among the most popular themes in animation.

Animation techniques make it possible to apparently bring to life objects of all kinds. In contrast to digital animation, the advantage of real objects which are manually animated—a printer scattering vinyl records onto a roll of paper, for example, or landscape collages for »Helmets« arranged by hand—is that the reality of these objects is never in doubt, in contrast to their virtually generated relatives. For these are real bodies in motion—albeit made of fabric, paper, modeling clay or tape.

Although the active intervention into this microcosm of objects is no longer visible in the finished film, each movement in the film betrays its genesis. And merely knowing about these manual manipulations enhances the astonishment and enjoyment of the viewer.

Thus the unique charm of stop-motion animation lies precisely in this characteristic of unveiling the illusion. Even if some effects are difficult to decipher, the process of stop-motion animation lays the construction of its illusionary worlds bare in a charmingly disarming fashion—and the laborious manual work is also clearly evident in the animated result.

In all this, the candid model origin in this filmic universe is never subjected to a striving for perfect illusions, nor is it exposed to the dangers of metaphorical exaggeration. The focus here is not on imitating reality, but on experimentation within these autonomous model worlds. As Heinz Edelmann's animated film »Yellow Submarine« demonstrated as far back as 1968, such model worlds are ideal vehicles for linking highly imaginative, fantasy-driven narratives. For the laws of physics, logic, and biology are easily set aside in animation. Any conceivable metamorphosis can be realized by hand—frame by frame.

In terms of the timeline, productions of this kind are defined by diametrically opposite coordinates: they are created between the extremes of a complete standstill and terrific speed. On the one hand, even dolly sequences at breakneck speed are in fact composed of a series of stills; on the other hand, the total length of the film rarely exceeds the length of a clip, while the production time for these short films can range anywhere from several days to many months. As in classic video clips, music provides the impulse and rhythm in most of the animated examples featured here. Music ensures that the symbols don't simply drift and tumble through space without any temporal reference, and is thus the only authority to which the world of objects liberated from all regulations does in fact respond. Its movements and formations are synchronized to the music, made possible by the universally applied digital editing technology.

When typography is introduced into this environment, the synchronization of motion and music must be simultaneously understood as a scenic representation of the lyrics. The simplest and also most famous example of this kind of typographical choreography is perhaps Bob Dylan's cameo in D.A. Pennebaker's classic documentary »Don't Look Back« where the singer holds up a series of cardboard sheets showing handwritten excerpts from the lyrics of his »Subterranean Homesick Blues«, casting each board aside as he moves on to the next line in a verse. Pennebaker's opener to »Don't Look Back« is today widely regarded as the first music video. It has been visually quoted numberless times by young pop bands throughout the world. In <u>Catrin Sonnabend's</u> [→ p. 197] music clip »Micronomic«, by contrast, type is liberated from its existence as part of the ensemble and assumes the role of interpreter and background dancer.

When real people do emerge within the works featured here, every now and then, they are less protagonists or lead actors than three-dimensional figures and image carriers, among other, constructed modules. In other words, the focus isn't on the human figure, even if it becomes the measure of all things when stripped of its personal expression. For it is only in relation to the human proportions that the true scale of the objects in the space can be ascertained with any certainty. The appearance of a hand or a whole person is thus an element of surprise when a backdrop is thereby suddenly revealed as a miniature model. Conversely, the arrangements within the space can be scaled up to oversized dimensions. An antagonizing or irritating change in proportions is a deliberate element in this approach. At the start of »Chelsea Girls« by <u>Peepshow</u> [→ p. 191], we see a person seated at a desk fashioning small cubes, triangles, and other geometrical shapes with craft paper and scissors. The same objects turn round and round on a paper plate in the foreground and converge into shifting tower sculptures, increasing in size to knee-high cartoons in the background.

The animation of symbols and objects abolishes the boundary between backdrop and protagonist. The material objects in the space become actors, and within this play they create shifting spatial and temporal structures. Unlike performance art, the choreography of symbols is executed without the presence of an audience and, furthermore, also without any claim to artistic authorship in the finished product.

One exception is the film »zZz is playing: Grip« by <u>Xelor / Roel Wouters</u> [→ p. 198] featured in this selection. It is unusual in several ways: the animation of the symbols, in this case represented by means of single-color square blocks of type with menu options for video effects, takes place in real time through the movement of real people jumping up and down on a trampoline. What's more, the clip was recorded on a one-shot setting, that is, without a single editing cut, from a bird's-eye perspective. Although the public isn't in the frame per se, it is witness to the entire action and is filmed by a second camera on the ground. Set to music, the film is realized without any tricks: every action is executed by real extras. Even the two band members and their instruments are pushed into view on dollies that are clearly visible from above. In order to perfectly transpose the symbols from the digital world into real action, a time-bar at the bottom of the screen is painted in throughout the entire clip. As befits this film, the painting is done by hand with a white paint roller and—seemingly by chance—the extra who »performs« this action reaches the end of the bar at precisely the same moment that the last trampoline jumper leaps out of frame. Nevertheless, this clip shares some basic features with the other 3-D animations presented here: the theme is a temporal and spatial staging of symbols. As planes and volumes collide, new formal constellations emerge that also render the space experiential in the virtual sphere.

In »Monsters« by Jean and Nicolas Jullien [→ p. 196], the two-dimensional sphere extends its shadowy arms into the real space, taking possession of the space and the two sleeping individuals in it by gliding over top of these three-dimensional bodies or completely enveloping them. The monster itself remains invisible; all we see are its arms, composed of black rolls of paper with serrated claws, having their way with the third dimension. In the video created by Us (Design Studio) [→ p. 193] for »Product Red«, the two-dimensional sphere spreads across the 3-D environment in a similar fashion: a real life single-family home is almost entirely covered in red tape. Once packaged in this manner, the tape-covered shape is endowed with a new graphic surface that renders the house abstract in an enchanting fashion.

How simple means—camera and editing technology aside—can be used to realize a dynamic treatment of space is demonstrated in the aforementioned music video »Micronomic«, filmed in stop-motion for the song of the same name by Lali Puna: to begin with, brown cardboard, colored paper, tape, and string form the shapes of graphic symbols and words on a concrete wall. As the video progresses, they leave the interior space and move out onto the street. We see the tape wandering along gutters and gullies, climbing over curbs and momentarily highlighting nondescript nooks in the urban space.

Might this be a postdigital revolt of symbols? In his essay »Kool Killer« from 1975, the French philosopher Jean Baudrillard ascribed the potency of early graffiti in New York to the fact that they do not communicate content or convey a message. Street Art tags penetrate the linguistic space of a decoded city in the form of significant voids. Formal references and overlaps between the free symbols of the subcultures and the object worlds of these examples that are set in motion would be easy to establish. Yet the experimental spatial arrangements of the sequences of symbols and the autonomy they assume do not make any territorial claims. They romp about within the sheltered and prepared space.

These works are a liberation: on the one hand, they are liberating for their creators, who gather and rejoice in letting their ideas flow freely as a team and by hand instead of at the click of a mouse—a tactile warm-up exercise, one might say—and on the other hand, they act as a temporary release from all economic constraints and limitations.

What remains is the scenographic experience, which is ultimately also collectivized with the help of the medium of film. We need to understand this performance of symbols as an expansion of the spatial and temporal capacity for imagination, which could not be realized in this form in any other medium.

Text: Sophia Muckle

JULIEN VALLÉE
↳53→106→207

BLACK & WHITE

Client: Bleublancrouge / Video & Photography: Julien Vallée
Music: René-Pierre Guérin

In »Black & White« by Julien Vallée the world of objects leaps out
from a pop-up book: the highly effective pop-up principle is further
enhanced by means of stop-motion animation. The tools used to
create the pop-up book scenarios circle around their own creations.

VIDEO: THREE-D.CH/BLACKWHITE

A NICE IDEA EVERY DAY
↳118→201

YOU, DOG (AKA KIDZ ARE SO SMALL) / DEERHOOF

Client: Deerhoof
Video: A Nice Idea Every Day with Piotr Petrovich

Within the clean ambience of the music video »You, Dog (AKA Kidz Are So Small)«, graphic elements and real objects are set in motion with such perfection that they are barely discernible from computer-generated animation. The handmade look of the paper objects, and the hands that appear in the frame every now and then, are the only indications of the analog creation process of the film. Indeed, everything was shot in stop-motion, even the smooth flowing movements of the white Styrofoam spheres that are suspended on invisible nylon threads.

VIDEO: THREE-D.CH/YOUDOG

TIM BROWN
↳130→201

A DIFFERENT VIEW / DEGREE SHOW

Client: Kingston University / Video: Tim Brown, Luke Taylor, Christopher Barrett, Kieren Dickens, Edward Heal, Kalvny French-James

Looking at things from a different perspective is an ability that is especially pronounced among young designers. In »A Different View«, a promotional film for Kingston University, Tim Brown's team illustrates the beneficial effects of an uninhibited point of view.

E4 MUSIC STINGS / DISCOGRAPHY

Client: E4 Music Channel
Video: Tim Brown and Fred Rigby

Since music no longer has to demonstrate tactile qualities in the age of the MP3, the LP still serves as its emblem. The recording medium becomes an image carrier symbolizing personal tastes in music as well as collective enjoyment of music: the very characteristics a music channel would like to offer to its listeners. In the »E4 Music Stings« video, LPs are therefore combined to form the logo of the E4 Music Channel.

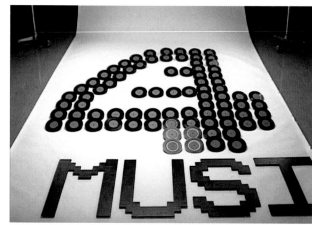

VIDEO: THREE-D.CH/DEGREESHOW

VIDEO: THREE-D.CH/E4

TIM BROWN
↳130→201

STYLE CRUSADER / BIG FACE

Client: City Rockers / Directed & Produced by: Tim Brown & Louis Chang
Edited by: James Wright / Photography: Tim Brown / Camera Crew: Garath Whyte

»Style Crusader«, the music video for Big Face, is all about the personal styles of the individual band members. Tim Brown and Louis Chang capture the different attitudes in photorealistic images and mount them onto white cubes, which, like the Rubik's cube, form ever-changing combinations and perspectives. The changing cube sculptures act as a visual equivalent of the eclectic sound of the band.

JENNIE HANCOCK
↳56→142→202

CAPTURING CREATIVITY

Client: Kodak Student Commerial Awards / Team: Ewan Robertson, Oscar Bauer, Jennie Hancock & Jonas Lund

Jennie Hancock's half-minute advertising spot for Kodak shows a designer with his head resting on a desk. What appears to be an apathetic state of exhaustion at first glance is revealed as the exact opposite to a creative crisis: a calm voice-over informs us that the human brain is at its most creative when in a state of complete relaxation. The ideas originating from the brain, made concrete in the form of three-dimensional shapes, circle around the imaginative head of the designer and can be captured with the help of the handy digital camera.

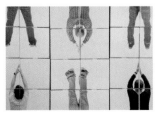

VIDEO: THREE-D.CH/BIGFACE

VIDEO: THREE-D.CH/KODAK

SWEDENGRAPHICS
↳108→166→206

MTV IDENTS 1–4 / TV CHANNEL IDENTITY

Client: MTV UK
Video: Swedengraphics

The image trailers for MTV do not display the logo of the music channel. Instead they intone the sound of the three initials through a filter of electronic distortion. The RGB colors for monitors (red, green, blue) drip from the ceiling, run down the chipboard panels leaning against walls, and pool into puddles of color on the floor, while a paper object flits through TV and fan. What is striking is the makeshift workshop atmosphere, which was chosen as a candid setting, whereas the animation of the colors and cloud sculptures is reminiscent of animated sequences in Monty Python's Flying Circus or in Heinz Edelmann's classic »Yellow Submarine«.

VIDEO: THREE-D.CH/MTV

PEEPSHOW
↳205

CHELSEA GIRLS / DAVID E. SUGAR

Client: Brik a Brak / Video: Peepshow
DOP: Ollie Jacomelli

The music video »Chelsea Girls« begins with its own »making of«: in live footage, viewers see a person making geometric shapes by hand. As the video continues, these shapes provide the backdrop for the singer, animated by means of stop-motion and edited to accompany the song with great precision. The combination of differing film techniques and shifts in proportion generates a graphic and live performance in which model and real worlds merge into one another.

TOYOTA ECHO

Client: Bleublancrouge / Video: Marie O'Connor & Luke Best (Peepshow)
Photography: Stephen Lenthall

»Toyota Echo« seems to provide a real glimpse of the work of a talented car designer: the virtuoso handling of cutter, scissors, and paper converges with an unfailing sense of color and form in an unstoppable abundance of ideas. The time-lapse effect applied to the sequence of individual frames shows the various car models in the form of handmade instant collages in a rapid succession of images devoid of any hint of high-tech. The car models are customized to match the individual style of the sporty woman driver, who finally steps into the finished car and speeds off into the distance.

BENOIT LEMOINE & CÉCILE BOCHE
↳126→204

THE WHITE DESK

Self-initiated Work
Video & Photography: Benoit Lemoine & Cécile Boche

Proof that not all designers are paralyzed by the fear of the white sheet is provided by the video »The White Desk« by Benoit Lemoine and Cécile Boche. No sooner does the designer sit down at the empty desk than the creative working process seems to get under way as if of its own volition. Conscious and intuitive acts merge into one another and demonstrate collaborative teamwork on different levels. In the form of a film-within-a-film, we see previously recorded hands, now projected onto the desk, carrying out a variety of typical activities and handing objects to their real-life, in-the-moment, counterparts. Lemoine dedicated the video to his mother, with the goal of showing her what the work of graphic designers entails.

COLORS AND THE KIDS
↳201

HELMETS

Self-initiated Work
Video: Colors and the Kids

The film »Helmets« was created within a 24-hour period as an internal workshop for Colors and the Kids (CatK). Because little time is usually set aside for ideas and projects like these, the creators were faced with the challenge of realizing the entire stop-motion film of the story—from scripting to cutting/editing and sound—within an extremely short period of time. In the film, a streetscape rolls over wall and floor, animated by objects and a human figure wearing a protective helmet.

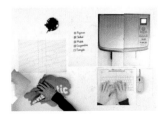 

VIDEO: THREE-D.CH/WHITEDESK

VIDEO: THREE-D.CH/HELMETS

US
↳207

PRODUCT RED

Client: Product Red
Video: Us Design Studio with Lee Davies

Initiated by U2 front man Bono and Bobby Shriver, Product Red is an umbrella label that sells limited editions of partner products such as Motorola, American Express, Apple, and many others under the Product Red logo. A percentage of the sales revenue is diverted to various humanitarian projects in Africa. The British design studio Us was commissioned to produce a highly visible and effective promo video aimed at the YouTube generation. To this end, Lee Davies and Luke Taylor wrapped a single-family house almost entirely in red tape, thus drawing attention to »red« products.

THOM YORKE / PROMO FOR »THE CLOCK«

Client: Thom Yorke
Video: Filmed by Garath Whyte and Kevin Williamson

Overtones of a critique of consumer consumption are translated into visual images in the promotional video for »The Clock« by Thom Yorke: in a minimally furnished white room, packaging waste threatens to destroy the purity of the space. After several attempts at hiding or obliterating the waste within his own four walls, the dispirited protagonist has the idea of using it to decorate the selfsame space. By creating a collage of garbage that grows along with to his consumption, he helps to give the throw-away materials new meaning.

VIDEO: THREE-D.CH/PRODUCTRED

VIDEO: THREE-D.CH/THECLOCK

JARED EBERHARDT
↳202

ALCOHOL / CANSAI DE SER SEXY

Client: Cansai De Ser Sexy, Sub Pop Records
Video: Jared Eberhardt

The music video »Alcohol« for the Brazilian band Cansai De Ser Sexy shows the musicians as eyeless rabbits made from modeling clay in a miniature landscape with a log cabin. An even smaller model of the band of rabbits enriches the scenery, the effect being that parallel worlds overlap more and more with reality as alcohol levels rise.

HIMSA

Client: Century Records
Video: Jared Eberhardt

In this music video, Jared Eberhardt transforms the band Himsa into hairy, monster-like dolls performing their song »Big Timber«. Hardcore rock 'n' rollers and their instruments cut loose in front of a nocturnal model landscape with a bizarre, morbid flora and a full moon. Dizzying camera scans through a tunnel of savage nature gradually converge into a narrative: once upon a time, the band built their instruments from raw materials found in the forest, which is now reclaiming the instruments and the materials. Eventually, tree stumps grow new limbs and the closing of the song is then performed by nature herself.

VIDEO: THREE-D.CH/CSS

VIDEO: THREE-D.CH/HIMSA

JARED EBERHARDT
↳202

VIDEO VINYL

Client: Imeem
Video: Jared Eberhardt

In the intro »Video Vinyl«, Jared Eberhardt, in the role of puppetmaster, animated an automated drum set made from modeling clay and glitter. It is a commonplace in the art of animation that automated processes or machines are in reality set in motion by small creatures—or, as is the case here—assume human characteristics.

LEGEND

Client: Legend, Title Sequence, Apple
Video: Jared Eberhardt

Real film sequences of snowboarders in action are shown on a homemade television screen as a realistic alpine landscape is being fashioned from paper in the background. Model world and real world are interchangeable in this clip, with typography being staged in accompaniment to the harsh swoosh of the snowboard.

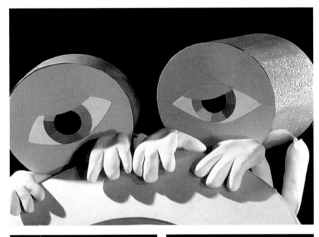

VIDEO: THREE-D.CH/VIDEOVINYL

VIDEO: THREE-D.CH/LEGEND

JEAN JULLIEN
↳33→203

THE NORMALITY ISSUE

Self-initiated Work / Film: Jean Jullien
Filmed in HDV. Direction and Script: Jean Jullien

Kafka reloaded: In the 50-minute film »The Normality Issue«, Jean Jullien uses bizarre images to tell the story of a boy who wakes up one day with a paper arm. Like Gregor Samsa in Kafka's famous story »The Metamorphosis«, absurdity takes on an apparent character of normalcy. Filmed in HDV. Written and directed by Jean Jullien.

MONSTERS

Self-initiated Work
Video: Jean Jullien & Nicolas Jullien

»Monsters«, a short film by Jean and Nicolas Jullien, plays with dimensions. The film was shot in two days with a DV camera. An apartment, which the filmmakers emptied in preparation for the shoot, is invaded by shadowy arms in the form of black handcut paper strips with serrated claws that take possession of the sleeping protagonist and the living space. These events are closely observed by black balloons with painted-on eyes, which populate the hallway. The film was realized with the simplest of means but is nevertheless gripping, especially because the »monster« named in the title is never fully visible, just its long arms.

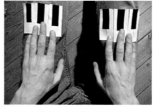

VIDEO: THREE-D.CH/NORMALITYISSUE

VIDEO: THREE-D.CH/MONSTERS

CATRIN SONNABEND
↳43→132→206

MICRONOMIC / LALI PUNA

Client: Lali Puna
Video & Photography: Catrin Sonnabend

»Micronomic« is a music video for the song of that name by the band Lali
Puna. The song describes the search for possibilities, paths, and goals.
It shows hesitant exploration and withdrawal, as well as uncertainty in
interaction with different options. This content is illustrated in trick
animation with graphic means that are as simple as they are abstract.

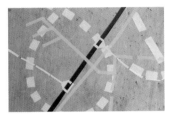

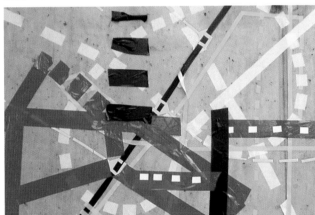
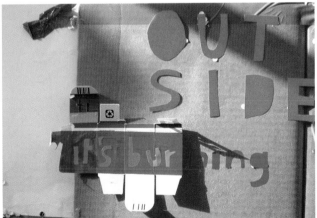

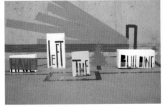

VIDEO: THREE-D.CH/MICRONOMIC

HORT
↳46→110→178→203

HORT SAYS HELLO / SHIFT COVER

Client: Shift.jp.org
Video: Hort

In the short typoclip, or typographic video clip, »Hort says hello«, the animation of emerging words composed of black rubber hoses bluntly declares their origin: the controlled staggering movement of the letters combined with the hand motions of a person who appears in the frame for a brief moment clearly shows that the letters are freely suspended within the space on thin nylon threads.

XELOR / ROEL WOUTERS
↳207

ZZZ IS PLAYING: GRIP

Client: Stedelijk Museum Den Bosch
Video: Xelor / Roel Wouters

»zZz is playing: Grip« by Xelor alias Roel Wouters, is a video in which the special effects of digital programs are transferred into a completely analog choreography. The entire clip was filmed live in front of an audience on a one-shot setting, that is, without a single cut or edit. From a bird's-eye perspective, the jumping surface of a trampoline appears as the work surface on a computer. On this surface, jumping gymnasts holding scoreboards simulate typical visual effects. To the side of this work surface, musicians are »rolled« into the frame, while the ubiquitous time bar at the bottom of the screen is painted in by hand. The clip was selected for inclusion in the »nederclips« exhibition at the Stedelijk Museum.

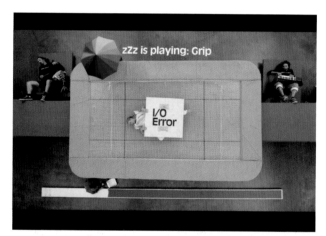

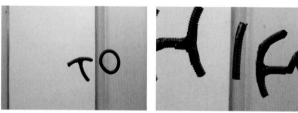

VIDEO: THREE-D.CH/HORT

VIDEO: THREE-D.CH/GRIP

XELOR / ROEL WOUTERS
↳207

ROBOT HIGH SCHOOL

Client: My Robot Friend / Video: Xelor / Roel Wouters
Production company: Goeroe media

The video »Robot High School« was created by the Dutch video artist
and designer Roel Wouters, who works under pseudonym Xelor.
Filmed on a one-shot setting like the previous example, the music video
shows a black ball in a landscape composed of black and white Op Art
patterns. The black ball encounters red balls and destroys them. Nothing remains of the red balls but bright red blots. The animation is
realized by rotating a cylinder [Drehwalze], cranked by a humanoid
robot. This process is somewhat reminiscent of filmic effects prior to rear
projection, when views of a landscape passing by as seen through the
windows of a driving car would be painted onto a large cylinder which
was rotated.

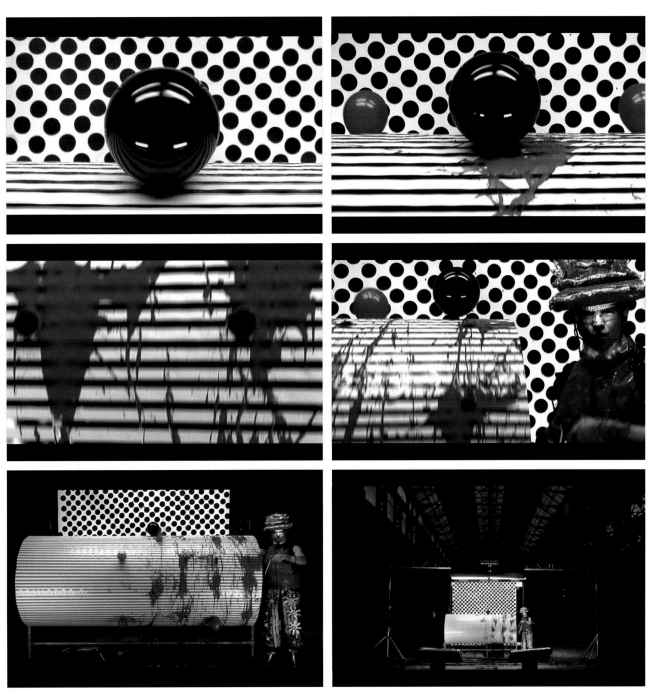

VIDEO: THREE-D.CH/ROBOT

→ # DESIGNERS AND STUDIOS

ANTOINE+MANUEL / WHY THREE D? »FOR EACH PROJECT WE BEGIN THE DESIGN PROCESS BY INVENTING AN ENTIRE SYSTEM OF FORMS, WITH ITS OWN VOCABULARY AND RULES. IN THIS PHASE OF CONCEPTUALIZING, WE FOCUS ON SHAPE AND ON THE STORY WE WANT TO TELL. WE ALWAYS KEEP IN MIND THAT THE OBJECTS WE CREATE ARE AIMED AT AN AUDIENCE, AND WE WANT TO PROVOKE EMOTIONS. SINCE WE ARE OUR FIRST AUDIENCE, THIS EMOTION HAS TO WORK ON US.«

A NICE IDEA EVERY DAY
WWW.ANICEIDEAEVERYDAY.COM /
CONTACT@ANICEIDEAEVERYDAY.COM
118→187

When Vivien Weyrauch and Fabian Röttger swing into action making videos and photographs, they do so under the promising name »A Nice Idea Every Day«. Vivien Weyrauch and Fabian Röttger live, work, and study in Dortmund.

GRÉGOIRE ALEXANDRE
WWW.GREGOIREALEXANDRE.COM
CONTACT@GREGOIREALEXANDRE.COM
88

Grégoire Alexandre was born in Rouen in 1972; he lives and works in Paris. A photographer, he completed his studies at the Université de Paris and the École Nationale Supérieure de la Photographie in Arles, and has since gone on to work in the fields of publishing, music, and advertising. His clients include Wallpaper*, Esquire UK, Yann Tiersen, Sony, and Citroën. Grégoire Alexandre has contributed works to group exhibitions in France, Spain, and Japan.

ANTOINE+MANUEL
WWW.ANTOINEETMANUEL.COM /
C@ANTOINEETMANUEL.COM
174

Antoine Audiau and Manuel Warosz met as students in Paris, and it was there that they began to collaborate under the name Antoine et Manuel. Since its beginnings, this artist duo has combined digital and handdrawn elements with photography and writing. Their clients include Christian Lacroix, Habitat, Galeries Lafayette, and Larousse.

ALEX BEC
WWW.ALEXBEC.COM / HELLO@ALEXBEC.COM
WWW.IFYOUCOULD.CO.UK
133

Alex Bec studied in Brighton; today he works in London as a freelance graphic designer, art director, and illustrator. In 2006, together with Will Hudson, he founded If You Could, a firm for creative projects in London's East End. Alex Bec is also a member of the design collective Peepshow.

TIM BROWN
WWW.TABROWN.CO.UK /
INFO@TABROWN.CO.UK
130→188

Since completing his studies at Kingston University, Tim Brown has worked in London as a freelance art director and designer. Following his present interests, the initiator of the magazine Lark regards film as the current focus of his work. His clients include Channel Four and the Paris Kitsuné label.

BYGGSTUDIO
WWW.BYGGSTUDIO.COM /
INFO@BYGGSTUDIO.COM
34→146

Hanna Nilsson, Markus Bergström, and Sofia Østerhus formed Byggstudio in 2006 after completing their studies at the Royal College of Art in London and the Copenhagen School of Design. Originally based in Copenhagen, the design studio recently moved its offices to Stockholm. In addition to pursuing their own independent projects, Hanna Nilsson and Sofia Østerhus also work in the areas of graphic design, illustration, and set and interior design for prominent clients throughout Scandinavia.

COLORS AND THE KIDS
WWW.COLORSANDTHEKIDS.COM /
HELLO@COLORSANDTHEKIDS.COM
192

Colors and the Kids (CatK) first went into action at Bauhaus University in Weimar, where Sebastian Gerbert, Maik Bluhm, and Elisabeth Schulze met in the course of their studies. Initially, they each took their own individual design paths, but the three of them later came together in Berlin to continue their joint work. Since then, CatK has given free rein to its creativity: from art direction and illustration to sound design, CatK works for small indepen-dent clients as well as large international firms Universal Music, Warner Music, Benetton, and many others.

BYGGSTUDIO / WHY THREE D? »WHEN WE STARTED WORKING TOGETHER, WE WERE TIRED OF THE OVERLOAD OF PHOTOSHOP COLLAGES SEEN IN MANY MAGAZINES. A SMOOTH PROCESS IS ALSO OF IMPORTANCE. WHEN WORKING WITH A CLIENT, WE FIRST GIVE THEM A COLLAGE-STYLE SKETCH IN ILLUSTRATOR OR PHOTOSHOP. SHOOTING, WE BRING OUR COLLECTION OF PROPS AND PLAY AROUND WITH COMPOSITION. WE TAKE THE PICTURE AND THE ONLY WORK LEFT IS A LITTLE RETOUCHING ON THE COMPUTER—NO TIME-CONSUMING EXPERIMENTS WITH LAYERS AND FILTERS ON THE SCREEN.«

COLORS AND THE KIDS / WHY THREE D? »DESIGNS THAT ARE DONE WITHOUT A COMPUTER ARE EXCITING, AND THE RESULTS ARE AS LIVELY AS THE PROCESS. IF YOU PAY ATTENTION, YOU CAN MAKE ERRORS AND ACCIDENTS PART OF THE WORK. WE ARE ESPECIALLY INTERESTED IN COMBINING WORKS IN REAL SPACE WITH THINGS PRODUCED ON THE COMPUTER TO GENERATE NEW VISUAL WORLDS.«

JOCELYN COTTENCIN

WWW.JOCELYNCOTTENCIN.COM /
CONTACT@JOCELYNCOTTENCIN.COM

143

It would be difficult to pigeonhole Jocelyn Cottencin in any particular movement or approach. Perhaps the best way to identify recurring elements in his work is to follow the trail of his varied and multifaceted production. One such facet, it would seem, is the use of writing. In Cottencin's work, letters are liable to turn into drawings or signs or become the basis for performative movements. Cottencin's works may be assigned with equal justification to the realms of art, design, and dance. Jocelyn Cottencin lives and works primarily in Rennes and otherwise wherever his projects happen to take him.

+41 //DIY

WWW.DIY.LI / DIY@DIY.LI /
PLUS41.CH / INFO@PLUS41.CH

40→97

The name of the Swiss design firm //DIY may be seen as an allusion to do-it-yourself practices—the working approach that is typically associated with them. With their own music and fashion label, these graduates of the École Cantonale d'Art de Lausanne are pursuing their declared objective of practicing design in the broadest possible sense. //DIY sees itself as a multidisciplinary platform with an emphasis on graphic design. In keeping with this vision, Laurence Jaccottet, Philippe Cuendet, and Ivan Liechti develop visual concepts independent of the medium in which they are realized.

EAT SLEEP WORK/PLAY

WWW.EATSLEEPWORKPLAY.COM /
ANTOINE@EATSLEEPWORKPLAY.COM /
ZAMIR@EATSLEEPWORKPLAY.COM

150

Eat Sleep Work/Play. What sounds like a fairly drab daily routine actually describes a design approach in which the strategy of play becomes the organizing principle. The members of the French-American design duo that goes by this name met as students at Central Saint Martins College of Art and Design in London. Since then, Eat Sleep Work/Play has been working on multidisciplinary projects (corporate identity, cover artwork, and publishing).

JARED EBERHARDT

WWW.JAREDEBERHARDT.COM /
JAREDE@MAC.COM

194

Instead of becoming a professional skater or snowboarder, Jared Eberhardt decided in the early 1990s to pursue a career as a photographer and designer. For years he worked for JDK Design and was the successful creative director for Burton Snowboards. From the very beginning of his career as a photographer, he has worked in nearly all design disciplines, from packaging design to film. The fact that his works consistently win prizes may have to do, among other things, with the athletic zeal he continues to bring to his projects.

EDHV

WWW.EDHV.NL /
INFO@EDHV.NL

153

For the design firm EDHV in the Dutch city of Eindhoven, established rules and boundaries are a welcome invitation to break and overcome them. For the designers at EDHV insist on giving every idea the freedom to develop. Allowing it the necessary time is an important part of the process, as are disparate perspectives and the shifting makeup of the teams.

BEN FREEMAN

WWW.BEN-FREEMAN.COM /
BEN@BEN-FREEMAN.COM

136

The British designer Ben Freeman lives in London, where he studied graphic design at Camberwell College of Art and the Royal College of Art. In addition to commissions for prominent clients such as Alexander McQueen, New Line Cinema, Ford, and Umbro, he also produces idiosyncratic independent works that may find him tattooing an eel, turning a gallery into a pinhole camera, or developing a visual system for the representation of feelings.

JENNIE HANCOCK

WWW.JENNIEHANCOCK.COM /
EMAIL@JENNIEHANCOCK.COM

56→142→189

In order to pursue her studies at Central Saint Martins College of Art and Design, Jennie Hancock moved from her home town of Liverpool to London. Since obtaining her degree, she has worked in London as a freelance graphic designer for Zip Design and others, as well as on various independent and commercial projects.

HVASS&HANNIBAL

WWW.HVASSHANNIBAL.DK /
INFO@HVASSHANNIBAL.DK /
WWW.MYSPACE.COM/HOVEDKONTORET /
WWW.NANNAHVASS.DK / WWW.SOFIEHANNIBAL.DK

98

The childhood playmates Nan Na and Sofie have gone on to become the Danish design duo Hvass&Hannibal, whose name sounds, in Danish, like the question »What's up Hannibal?« In the last two years, Hvass&Hannibal have designed countless flyers, posters, and T-shirts. In future, they are set to expand into the realms of music, video, and fashion, and at some point these students are sure to finish their studies at the Danish School of Design.

EAT SLEEP WORK/PLAY / WHY THREE D? »LET'S START WITH A SIMPLE ESTHETIC OBSERVATION: WHY DO A MAJORITY OF GRAPHIC DESIGNERS SYSTEMATICALLY CHOOSE TO PHOTOGRAPH THEIR WORK? THIS TECHNIQUE OF DOCUMENTATION WAS ALMOST ABSENT IN THE NINETIES. THE ›VECTOR‹ GENERATION PREFERRED TO DISPLAY THE GRAPHICS DIRECTLY ON SCREEN, FROM SCREEN TO SCREEN, SO TO SPEAK. THE OUTPUT DICTATED THE WORKING PROCESSES. THEN CAME DIGITAL PHOTOGRAPHY AS A TURNING POINT IN THE WAY GRAPHIC DESIGNERS PRESENT THEIR WORK. SURFING THE INTERNET REMINDS US OF THE SHEER NUMBER OF PRACTITIONERS EMERGING EVERYDAY ON THE WEB. CONTEMPORARY DESIGNERS SHOW THEIR WORK UNDER THE LENS OF THEIR DIGITAL CAMERA, *IN SITU*.«

BEN FREEMAN / WHY THREE D? »I GREW UP LOVING BOOKS, POSTERS, FLYERS, AND RECORD COVERS. THESE ARE NOT DIGITAL FILES, COLLECTIONS OF ZEROS AND ONES, THEY ARE PHYSICAL OBJECTS, AND IN THIS SENSE I SEE A BLUR IN THE LINE BETWEEN PRODUCT DESIGN AND GRAPHIC DESIGN. WHAT APPEALS IS THE TEXTURE, THE WEIGHT, AND THE SMELL OF AN OBJECT.«

HORT
WWW.HORT.ORG.UK /
CONTACT@HORT.ORG.UK
46→110→178→198
INTERVIEW PAGE 47

Today, the Berlin design studio Hort, which was originally called »Eikes grafischer Hort« (»Eike's Graphic Refuge«) after its founder, Eike König, is still what it was intended to be from the beginning: a creative playground where designers are able to run riot with their ideas. Originally, Hort primarily worked for record labels; it has since become an institution for multidisciplinary projects for such clients as Nike and other big players.

SARAH ILLENBERGER
WWW.SARAHILLENBERGER.COM /
INFO@SARAHILLENBERGER.COM
72

Sarah Illenberger is extremely versatile and adaptable: she turns subjects and ideas into highly evocative and unusual images and signs. Always in search of suitable materials—the perfect arrangement—Sarah Illenberger takes real objects and arranges them into surreal objects and sculptures for her illustrations. In her Berlin studio, she develops visual ideas and concepts for editorial departments and independent advertising projects.

JEAN JULLIEN
WWW.JEANJULLIEN.COM /
JEAN.JULLIEN@GMAIL.COM
33→196

Always in search of new design challenges, the London-based graphic designer Jean Jullien works in the fields of print, film, photography, and illustration. His many clients include Central Saint Martins, Cliché London, Amon Ray, Niwouinwouin, and Kitsune noir.

PHILIPPE JARRIGEON
WWW.MIKROSHOW.COM /
PHILIPPE@MIKROSHOW.COM
62→104

A graduate of the École Cantonale d'Art de Lausanne, Philippe Jarrigeon reveals unusual aspects of everyday life. Jarrigeon works for architects and industrial and fashion designers such as Adrien Rovero, Stéphane Barbier-Bouvet, Martin Margiela, and Gaspard Yurkievich. He lives and works in Paris.

FLORIAN JENETT
WWW.FLORIANJENETT.DE / WWW.PROCESSING.ORG
MAIL@FLORIANJENETT.DE
145

Equally at home in a number of different disciplines, Florian Jenett shifts back and forth between real and virtual worlds with great virtuosity. In addition to staging actions—such as handing out handguns made of ice in downtown Frankfurt, or car-tuning accessories ironically sculpted out of cardboard—Florian Jenett also works on the continued development of the programming language Processing, which was created for artists and designers at the MIT Media Lab. In 2006, Jenett, who is a graduate of the Academy of Art and Design Offenbach, co-founded the artists' network »basis« in Frankfurt am Main. Florian Jenett is also a lecturer at the University of Applied Sciences in Mainz.

KONG
WWW.KONG.CH /
WIR@KONG.CH
28→158

In a certain sense, the group Kong, which has its offices in the Swiss city of Biel, stands in the tradition of modern Swiss graphic design. The role of form is to follow function. The designers, however, do not rest content with historical citations, but also experiment with contemporary styles and methods. In addition to craftsmanship and a clear conception, design intuition also plays an important role in their work.

JEAN JULLIEN / WHY THREE D? »THERE'S SOMETHING REALLY SINCERE WITHIN THE OBJECTS AND TOOLS THAT I USE IN MY PICTURES TO GIVE A FEEL OF SIMPLICITY TO MY WORK. IN A SENSE, IT'S A WAY TO PUT ASIDE ALL THE VIRTUAL AND UNBELIEVABLE AND TO TRY TO SEDUCE AND ATTRACT BY MAKING THE MOST OF WHAT'S AROUND US: FLAWED BUT CHARMING MATERIALS. I DON'T THINK WE CAN SAY THAT IT'S ABOUT FINDING A NEW ESTHETIC; IT HAS NOTHING TO DO WITH A ›STYLE,‹ IF YOU ASK ME. IT'S ABOUT TRYING THINGS, EXPERIMENTING, AND FINDING NEW USES FOR THINGS.«

KÖRNER UNION
WWW.KOERNERUNION.COM /
CHOSES@KOERNERUNION.COM
54→107

In 1999, while still students at the École Cantonale d'Art de Lausanne, Sami Benhadj, Tarik Hayward, and Guy Meldem formed the group Körner Union. Since then, they have gone on to become a design firm that preserves its freedom for artistic experimentation.

EDHV / WHY THREE D? »DESIGNING ALSO MEANS KNOWING WHEN NOT TO DESIGN. AT EDHV WE FOCUS ON RESEARCH AND CONCEPT BEFORE EVEN THINKING ABOUT HOW TO DESIGN. THIS LEAVES OPEN ALL POSSIBILITIES UNTIL LATE IN THE PROCESS AND LEADS TO SURPRISING RESULTS, DRASTIC TURNS AND BIZARRE DISCOVERIES. SOMETHING YOU WOULD NEVER HAVE THOUGHT OF AT THE START OF A PROJECT. THINGS LIKE THAT ONLY HAPPEN IF YOU CAN FIND THE COURAGE TO LET GO OF THE CONTROL FACTOR, ›THE SAFE PATH,‹ AND EMBARK ON A JOURNEY INTO UNKNOWN TERRITORY. ERROR, FAILURE, COINCIDENCE, AND FLAWS ARE CRUCIAL INGREDIENTS OF OUR CREATIVE PROCESS.«

ELISABETH MOCH / WHY THREE D? »I HAVE ALWAYS LIKED TO WORK WITH MY HANDS, TO FEEL AND TOUCH DIFFERENT MATERIALS. FOR ME THIS IS THE MOST HONEST WAY TO APPROACH A SUBJECT. PHOTOSHOP IS A MAGICAL TOOL THAT I USE TO ROUND OUT A PIECE OR DELETE SMALL MISTAKES, BUT THOSE ACTIONS MUST NEVER BE RECOGNIZABLE. I LIKE IT WHEN A CREATION TAKES TIME AND WOULD SAY THAT ENDURANCE IS THE MOST STRIKING CHARACTERISTIC OF ALL MY WORKS. BESIDES, I GET EASILY BORED WITH THINGS AND PLAYING WITH TECHNIQUE OR MATERIAL SURELY PUMPS THE BLOOD BACK TO THE HEART.«

PEEPSHOW
WWW.PEEPSHOW.ORG.UK /
INFO@PEEPSHOW.ORG.UK
58→191

For about five years now, the design collective Peepshow from London's East End has been shaking up the creative scene in Britain. With a reputation for surprising and intelligent work, Peepshow is active in many different areas. Each of its twelve members contributes his or her own skills and experiences from a variety of different disciplines. Their projects cover a broad spectrum, from art direction and video to fashion and set design. Their clients include Ogilvy and Mather, M+C Saatchi, BBC, Coca-Cola, Diesel, and MTV.

PIXELGARTEN / WHY THREE D? »WE ARE INTERESTED IN THE BOUNDARIES BETWEEN THE MEDIA: THE TRANSITION FROM PHOTOGRAPHY TO GRAPHICS; ILLUSTRATIONS THAT IN TURN BECOME INSTALLATIONS. WE ARE LOOKING FOR WHAT LIES IN BETWEEN.«

PIXELGARTEN
WWW.PIXELGARTEN.DE /
HALLO@PIXELGARTEN.DE

Pixelgarten is a studio for interdisciplinary creation based in Frankfurt am Main and established in 2004 by Catrin Altenbrandt and Adrian Niessler, who met while studying visual communication at the Academy of Art and Design Offenbach. Their work is as humorous as it is poetic, often with a surreal aura and frequently full of allusions. But the working methods of this creative pair differ: whereas Altenbrandt tackles a task in a freer, more intuitive manner, Niessler's approach is more conceptual. They are both inspired by what is happening in the street, so to speak: absurd everyday events. Pixelgarten's work has been widely exhibited.

PLAYAREA
WWW.PLAY-AREA.CO.UK /
INFO@PLAY-AREA.CO.UK
114→180

Playarea is the London-based design firm of Hannah Draper and Mat Fowler. Founded in 2001, Playarea works for Carhartt, Silas & Maria, Girl, and Blueprint Skateboards and has also taken over art direction for the Pointer shoe label.

PLEASELETMEDESIGN
WWW.PLEASELETMEDESIGN.COM /
OH@PLEASELETMEDESIGN.COM
102→169

In 2004, after completing their studies at the École supérieure des beaux-arts in Liège and spending a year at the École de Recherche Graphique in Brussels, Pierre Smeets and Damien Aresta came together to form the Brussels design firm Pleaseletmedesign. In keeping with their motto, »Graphic design and everything else«, Pleaseletmedesign designs books, posters, Web sites, and exhibitions.

DAMIEN POULAIN
WWW.DAMIENPOULAIN.COM /
HELLO@DAMIENPOULAIN.COM
38→148

Before settling in London's East End in 2003, the French art director and graphic artist Damien Poulain already had working trips to Germany, Spain, and Italy behind him. A specialist in print media, he designs books, posters, and public relations materials for galleries and music and fashion labels. As a sideline, however, he also designs prints for T-shirts, Web sites, and spatial scenarios for magazines such as »Tank« and »Arena Homme+«.

RITA
WWW.RITARITARITA.CA /
RITA@RITARITARITA.CA
116

Concealed behind the somewhat old-fashioned sounding woman's name »Rita« lies the view of this Montreal-based Canadian design firm that different design disciplines are capable of inspiring and cross-pollinating each other at a fundamental level. The symbiosis of different perspectives and ways of working leads designers Karine Corbeil, Stéphane Halmaï-Voisard, and Francis Rollin to new formal and functional approaches.

PLEASELETMEDESIGN / WHY THREE D? »IT'S PART OF OUR PROCESS TO GO STRAIGHT TO THE ESSENTIALS. WORKING IN 3-D IS CLOSER TO OUR ›VISION‹ OF GRAPHIC DESIGN, MAINLY FOCUSED ON STRONG CONCEPTS. WHEN WE DO IT FOR REAL, IT IS THE BEST WAY TO GIVE LIFE TO OUR IDEAS. IT'S SIMPLER AND MORE IMMEDIATE. EVERY PROJECT IS THOUGHT THROUGH AND SKETCHED BEFORE STARTING ANY ›COMPUTERIZATION‹.«

VALENTIN RUHRY
WWW.RUHRY.COM /
VALENTIN@RUHRY.AT
117

Valentin Ruhry uses everyday objects such as gym shoes, light bulbs, and power strips in his works. One might easily conclude that the works of this graduate of the University of Applied Arts Vienna are ready-mades—were it not for the fact that they are actually exact reproductions of everyday objects.

KATRIN SCHACKE
WWW.KATRINSCHACKE.DE /
HALLO@KATRINSCHACKE.DE
92

In her works, the graphic designer Katrin Schacke combines her real environment with the world of graphic signs and symbols, always in search of the dramatic potential that material and space have to offer. Whether it be the projection of film stills on the surface of a pool or a portrait of thousands of petals, this graduate of the Academy of Art and Design Offenbach is intent on creating new visual impressions.

KATRIN SCHACKE / WHY THREE D? »IMAGES OFTEN DERIVE PERSONALITY PRECISELY FROM LITTLE FLAWS IN THE OBJECTS THEY FEATURE, BACKGROUND DETAILS THAT SUPPOSEDLY DISTURB THE WORK, AND ELEMENTS THAT INTRUDE INTO THE IMAGE, SEEMINGLY BY MISTAKE. OFTEN TOO, MOVEMENT—AND HENCE CHANCE—CREATES A WHOLLY INDIVIDUAL PICTORIAL CHARACTER THAT WOULD BE IMPOSSIBLE TO GENERATE ON A COMPUTER.«

VALERIE SIETZY
VA-RI@GMX.DE
112

In her works, this graduate of the Academy of Art and Design Offenbach uses familiar everyday objects, which she places in new contexts to provoke unaccustomed associations. She surprises the viewer with design interventions in the urban public realm that transform banal sites and invest them with additional levels of meaning.

CATRIN SONNABEND
WWW.CATRINSONNABEND.DE /
HALLO@CATRINSONNABEND.DE
43→132→197

Catrin Sonnabend completed her studies at the Academy of Art and Design Offenbach. She has received numerous prizes for her work. She now works in Frankfurt, New York, and Berlin as a freelance graphic designer.

REBECCA STEPHANY
WWW.REBECCASTEPHANY.COM /
MAIL@REBECCASTEPHANY.COM
162

Rebecca Stephany lives and works in Amsterdam. After studying at the Academy of Art and Design Offenbach and the Gerrit Rietveld Academy in Amsterdam, she accepted a teaching post at the Gerrit Rietveld Academy; she works in the areas of illustration and publishing both in and outside Amsterdam.

JULIETTE TINNUS / WHY THREE D? »FOR ME, HAPTIC DESIGN IN THREE-DIMENSIONAL SPACE IS MORE SENSUOUS AND MORE FULFILLING, BUT OFTEN ALSO MORE CHALLENGING, SINCE OBJECTS CANNOT BE TWISTED AND ARRANGED AS EASILY AS VECTORS ON A COMPUTER. BUT THAT, I THINK, IS PRECISELY WHAT MAKES FOR THE QUALITY AND MAGIC OF THE IMAGES.«

STILETTO NYC
WWW.STILETTONYC.COM /
INFO@STILETTONYC.COM
65

Stiletto NYC, with offices in New York and Milan, is a design firm specializing in art direction in the fields of print and video. Founded in 2000 by Stefanie Barth and Julie Hirschfeld, Stiletto NYC works for clients on both sides of the Atlantic, including MTV, Condé Nast, Nike, Samsung, Lamarthe, and various boutiques in Europe and the United States.

SWEDENGRAPHICS / WHY THREE D? »I THINK IT IS A WAY OF BRINGING AN ELEMENT OF CHANCE INTO YOUR DESIGN. YOU DO NOT HAVE FULL CONTROL AND THEREFORE IT FEELS LIKE YOU DO NOT HAVE FULL RESPONSIBILITY EITHER, WHICH CAN BE VERY RELAXING. ACTUALLY I THINK MAYBE IT HAS MORE TO DO WITH USING A CAMERA THAN WITH THE ACTUAL 3-D-ING. WHEN YOU ARE USING A CAMERA YOU BECOME MORE A KIND OF OBSERVER THAN CREATOR. YOU ARE DOCUMENTING SOMETHING RATHER THAN CREATING IT. AND YOU CAN OFTEN GET A FEELING THAT IT IS ONLY AFTER DOING THE WHOLE SHOOT THAT YOU UNDERSTAND WHAT IT IS YOU WANTED TO DO ALL ALONG. AND THEN IT IS TOO LATE!«

SWEDENGRAPHICS
WWW.SWEDENGRAPHICS.COM /
HELLO@SWEDENGRAPHICS.COM
108→166

Since completing their studies in 1997, Nille Svensson and Magnus Åström have joined forces in Stockholm under the name Swedengraphics. Their clients include such companies as H&M, Sony, Ebay, and VW as well as numerous Swedish clients. Their works have been published in various international magazines. They also founded the Swedish art magazine Konstnären and the publishing house Pocky. Nille Svensson's work as a teacher has taken him to Tijuana and Sydney.

JULIETTE TINNUS
WWW.JULIETTETINNUS.COM /
HELLO@JULIETTETINNUS.COM
68

After receiving her diploma of business management, Juliette Tinnus studied visual communication with an emphasis on fine art and photography at the Academy of Art and Design Offenbach. Toward the end of her studies, she moved to San Francisco, where she lives and works today. In her photographs, Juliette Tinnus arranges strange objects and decorative elements into original compositions.

UNDERWARE
WWW.UNDERWARE.NL /
WWW.TYPEWORKSHOP.COM
172

Underware is a Dutch graphic design studio founded in 1999 by Akiem Helmling, Bas Jacobs and Sami Kortemäki which is specialized in designing and producing typefaces. The website www.typeworkshop.com origines from workshops given by the designers in recent years. They are always looking for more people to cooperate. Every idea and proposal is welcome, just send them an e-mail.

UNTITLED2
WWW.UNTITLED2.COM / VANCE@UNTITLED2.COM
WWW.MAKINGKNOWN.ORG / RYAN@MAKINGKNOWN.ORG
181

Ryan Nelson and Vance Wellenstein met at DesignWorks, the internal design firm of the Minneapolis College of Art and Design, which is run by students and alumni of the college. While at DesignWorks, the two graphic designers worked together on commissions as well as on projects of their own.

ELENE USDIN / WHY THREE D? »IT BEGAN WHEN I WAS A LITTLE GIRL WITH MY GRANDMOTHER WHO TAUGHT ME TO KNIT. ONE DAY A SEWING MACHINE CAME INTO MY LIFE AND I BEGAN TO GET CRAZY ABOUT CREATING THINGS WITH FABRICS AS A WAY TO REINTERPRET REAL THINGS WITH AN UNUSUAL USE OF MATERIAL. WOOL FOR TEARS, PLASTIC FOR RAIN, FABRICS FOR FRUITS OR A SKELETON. IT TAKES ME A LONG TIME TO PREPARE EVERYTHING BEFORE THE SHOOT AND FIX UP THE SET THE DAY OF SHOOTING, EVEN IF EVERYTHING IS PREPARED AND CAL-CULATED. I LOVE TO THINK THAT PEOPLE MIGHT SEE IMPERFECTION AND HAZARD IN IT.«

US
WWW.USDESIGNSTUDIO.CO.UK /
INFO@USDESIGNSTUDIO.CO.UK
193

The London design firm Us was founded by Christopher Barrett, Edward Heal, and Luke Taylor. However, they do not see their inter-disciplinary design approach as being a result of artistic freedom, but as the logical con-sequence of the service orientation around which their work is organized.

ELENE USDIN
WWW.ELENEUSDIN.COM / ELENE@HARTLANDVILLA.COM
REPRESENTED BY WWW.VALERIEHERSLEVEN.COM
82

Elene Usdin completed her studies at the École des Arts Decoratifs in Paris and then began to work as an illustrator for magazines and books. She only discovered her passion for the medium of photography in 2003, when she began to experiment with self-portraits. Her series of self-portraits won the Picto Prize for Young Fashion Photography, although they were not, strictly speaking, fashion photographs.

JULIEN VALLÉE
WWW.JVALLEE.COM /
J@JVALLEE.COM
53→106→186

As a freelance art director and motion and graphic designer, Julien Vallée has made a name for himself from Montreal to Paris and Los Angeles. His frequent moves and the associated shifts in perspective have no doubt sharpened his eye for the things around him.

PIERRE VANNI
WWW.PIERREVANNI.COM /
PVANNI@HOTMAIL.FR
57→73→185

Pierre Vanni draws his inspiration from con-temporary art and art-historical subjects. This graphic designer and art director, who earned his Master at the Université de Toulouse le Mirail with a thesis on the return of tactile qualities in the applied arts, derives his design approach from minimalist concepts and uses reduction to lend concision to his works.

XELOR / ROEL WOUTERS
WWW.XELOR.NL /
ROEL@XELOR.NL
198

As an artist, designer, and filmmaker, Roel Wouters deals with interpersonal relation-ships. His protagonists' desire for structure often leads to compulsions, which Wouters makes visible in his works through targeted deconstruction or deliberate manipulation. He lives in Amsterdam, works under the pseudonym Xelor, and teaches at the Gerrit Rietveld Academy and the Sandberg Institute. As a filmmaker, he works for such companies as Goeroemedia (the Netherlands) and Nexus Productions (international). Currently, Wouters is working with Luna Maurer, Edo Paulus, and Jonathan Puckey on the »Condi-tional Design Manifesto«, which will describe his artistic position.

UNTITLED2 / WHY THREE D? »CONSID-ERING THE PHYSICAL SIZE AND THE RANGE OF CON-TENT, A DIMENSIONAL WORKING SPACE CREATED MORE VISUAL OPPORTU-NITY THAN A COMPOSI-TION RELYING STRICTLY ON TYPE AND IMAGE WITHIN A GRID. ATTEMPTING TO BREAK WITH CONVENTION, WE STEPPED AWAY FROM THE SYSTEMATIC NATURE OF THE COMPUTER TO PHOTOGRAPH A ›DESIGNED ENVIRONMENT.‹ THIS ALLOWED US TO FIND A SOLUTION THAT WAS MORE DYNAMIC, INVOLVED, AND DEFINED BY INTRICACIES NOT TYPICALLY FOUND IN THE DIGITAL REALM.«

This book is also available in a German language edition
(ISBN: 978-3-7643-8770-9).

Library of Congress Control Number: 2008932839

Bibliographic information published by the German
National Library
The German National Library lists this publication in the
Deutsche Nationalbibliografie; detailed bibliographic
data are available on the Internet at http://dnb.d-nb.de.

© 2009 Birkhäuser Verlag AG
P.O. Box 133, CH-4010 Basel, Switzerland
Part of Springer Science+Business Media

© 2009 ProLitteris, Zurich for the reproduced work
by Peter Blake

Idea and Design: Pixelgarten
Photo (Cover): Christiane Feser + Pixelgarten
Texts: Sophia Muckle
Text Editor: Nora Kempkens
Litho: lithotronic media GmbH

Translation from German into English:
Elizabeth Schwaiger, Toronto (essays and captions)
Steven Lindberg, Berlin (interviews)
Jim Gussen, Sommerville/MA (index)
Copy editing: Susan James, Etobicoke, ON

Printed on acid-free paper produced from chlorine-free
pulp TCF ∞

Printed in Germany
ISBN: 978-3-7643-8771-6

9 8 7 6 5 4 3 2 1
www.birkhauser.ch